FIRST AID
HANDBOOK

FIRST AID
HANDBOOK

A complete guide to emergency procedures
in the home, the workplace, and outdoors

CONSULTANT EDITOR
Dr Susan Lipscombe

AUTHOR
Anita Kerwin-Nye

This is a Parragon Publishing Book

First published in 2005

Parragon Publishing
Queen Street House
4 Queen Street
Bath BA1 1HE, UK

Copyright © Parragon 2004

Printed in Indonesia

Created and produced for Parragon Publishing by
THE BRIDGEWATER BOOK COMPANY LIMITED

ISBN 1-40545-481-4

The views expressed in this book are those of the author but they are general views only
and readers are urged to consult a relevant and qualified specialist for individual advice in
particular situations. The publishers hereby exclude all liability to the extent permitted by law
for any errors or omissions in this book and for any loss, damage, or expense (whether direct
or indirect) suffered by a third party relying on any information obtained in this book.

It is advised that this book provides a reference for first aid techniques and that first aid
should always be carried out by a trained first responder.

Contents

First Aid Techniques

At the Emergency Scene

When faced with an emergency situation, you should follow a set routine and establish your priorities. If possible, send someone to call for medical help while you deal with the situation. Make sure that you are in no danger and make the scene safe. Then check the victim's condition and carry out treatment as appropriate.

GETTING APPROPRIATE HELP Life-threatening emergencies require professional medical assistance. If possible, ask a bystander to contact the emergency services by dialling 911. Useful information to have at hand includes:

- Details of what happened.
- Number of people injured.
- Type of illness or injuries.
- Whether or not person is breathing.
- The exact address with landmarks if possible.
- A contact phone number.

Do not hang up until the operator tells you to. He or she may be able to guide you through first aid procedures if you are unsure what to do next.

MAKING THE SCENE SAFE The cardinal rule of first aid is to ensure that you can give assistance without endangering yourself. Do not rush to the scene: walk slowly and steadily, looking around you for potential dangers and an overview of what has happened. Be prepared to take charge unless someone more qualified than you is present. Identify dangers and remove them if it is safe to do so, but if you cannot eliminate the danger, call for emergency help and advice and consider whether the danger poses a continuing risk to the injured person. If it does, assess whether you can safely move him or her. If in doubt, do not approach the scene. Keep everybody else back and call for emergency help.

Potential dangers include:
- At the scene of an accident—other cars, broken glass or metal, or an unsteady crash vehicle.
- Chemicals, fire, or electricity.
- Aggressive behavior in those who may be ill, hysterical, or as a result of drugs or alcohol.
- Sharp objects on the floor such as a knife or syringe.

TREATING THE INJURED OR ILL If you can give first aid safely, your priorities are to maintain an open airway and resuscitate if necessary, to treat serious bleeding and to treat for shock. If faced with several injured people,

Left

When a person is unconscious he is at risk of the airway becoming blocked by the tongue. To keep the airway open, place the victim on his back, and open the airway by tilting the head and lifting the chin.

always approach the quietest first—a person who is shouting is at least able to maintain a clear airway.

Determining what may be wrong with an injured person is part of the treatment. To help you reach a provisional diagnosis you need to consider:

● What actually happened (from what you or a bystander has observed).

● The signs (what you can see, hear, touch, or smell on the victim such as pale skin, swelling, noisy breathing, or alcohol on the breath).

● The symptoms (what the injured or ill person tells you—for example, he or she feels dizzy or is in pain).

First aid by its very nature is often a highly emotional activity. It is important that, after helping at the scene of the accident, you give yourself the chance to discuss what happened, what you did and how you feel with your family and friends.

Above

To see if a person who has collapsed is still conscious, squeeze the shoulders gently (because the neck may be injured), and ask the person if he is all right. Speak loudly and clearly.

Below

While waiting for help to arrive, place the victim in the recovery position. This keeps the airway open and allows fluid to flow out of the mouth if the victim vomits.

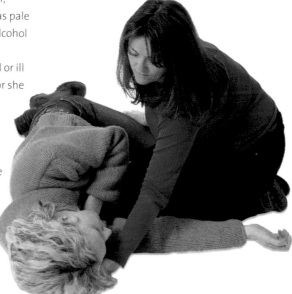

Action in an Emergency

Is anyone in danger?

Move to the quietest victim first

✚ If yes, can the danger be easily managed?

✚ If it cannot, call for emergency help and protect the scene.

✚ Gently shake the shoulders and ask him or her a question.

✚ If there is a response, treat any life-threatening condition before checking the next person.

✚ If there is no response, check the airway.

If not breathing

✚ Give 2 rescue breaths by pinching the nose, sealing your mouth over his or her mouth, and breathing into the person.

✚ If you are alone, call for an ambulance as soon as you determine that the victim is not breathing.

If breathing

✚ Check for and treat any life-threatening conditions and place in the recovery position.

Open the airway

+ Lift the chin, check the mouth for any obstructions and remove, then tilt the head back gently.

Check for breathing

+ Place your cheek close to his or her mouth and listen and feel for breathing. Look to see if the chest is moving.

Look for signs of circulation

+ If the victim is a child, or an adult who has suffered drowning or an accident, proceed direct to CPR (cardiopulmonary resuscitation).

+ Otherwise look for signs of life such as movement and normal skin color for 10 seconds.

Continue Rescue Breathing

+ Check for signs of circulation every minute.

Start CPR
(cardiopulmonary resuscitation)

+ Combine rescue breathing with chest compressions.

Assessing a Victim

Prompt action during an emergency could mean the difference between life and death. The following article describes how to assess a victim's airway and breathing. For further information, see pages 14–17.

CHECK THE RESPONSE If faced with a person who appears to be unresponsive, check the response by gently shaking the shoulders and asking loudly, "Are you all right?" Speak loudly and clearly and squeeze gently because there may be a neck injury.

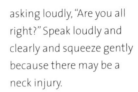

OPEN THE AIRWAY

1 Place one hand on the forehead and gently tilt the head back. Open the victim's mouth and remove any obvious obstructions, including dislodged dentures, but leave well-fitting dentures in place.

2 Place the fingertips of the other hand under the point of the victim's chin and lift the chin. If injury to the neck is suspected, handle the head very gently and try to avoid tilting the head.

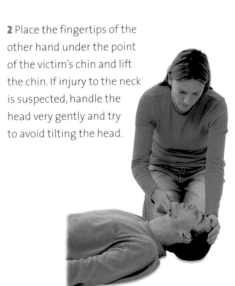

IF THERE IS NO RESPONSE Shout for help. If possible, leave the victim in the position in which you found him and open the airway. When it is not possible to carry out an assessment of the victim in the position found, turn the person onto his back and open the airway.

Apply the same techniques for a child as for an adult. For a baby, use only one finger under the chin and be very careful not to over-extend the neck when tilting the head back.

CHECK FOR BREATHING Keep the airway open and look, listen, and feel for breathing for no more than 10 seconds.

- Look for chest movement.
- Listen for sounds of breathing.
- Feel for breath on your cheek.

Look, listen, and feel for breathing for no more than 10 seconds

SIGNS AND SYMPTOMS OF A NON-BREATHING CASUALTY

- Unconsciousness, stillness.
- Pale skin with possible blue lips.
- No movement of the chest.
- No feeling or sound of breathing.

OPENING AIRWAY AND CHECKING BREATHING

Assessing a baby or toddler
If the victim is a toddler or a baby, it is important to handle them with care. Roll the baby gently onto its back with one hand, making sure you cradle the head with the other. To open the airway, place only one finger under the chin and tilt the head back slowly. Do not tip the head back too far as this may cause damage to the neck. Once you are sure the airway is clear, check for breathing for no more than ten seconds.

✔ **DO**	❓ **WHAT IF**
• Check to see if the victim is conscious. • Open the airway by gently lifting the chin, checking in the mouth, and tilting the head. • Check for breathing for up to 10 seconds.	• The person is unconscious? Treat any other injuries as necessary. • The person is breathing? Turn into the recovery position (see pages 20–23). • The person is not breathing? Give rescue breaths (see pages 24–27).

DO NOT	
• Sweep blindly in the mouth for obstructions.	

Maintaining Airway, Breathing, and Circulation

The most important principle of first aid is the ABC of resuscitation, which stands

for Airway, Breathing, and Circulation. This is a life-saving procedure that will enable

you to decide whether a victim who has collapsed needs rescue breathing or CPR

(cardiopulmonary resuscitation). The airway must be open, breathing must be checked,

and circulation must be assessed. Always follow the ABC sequence before giving any other

treatment if the victim is unconscious.

RESUSCITATION Resuscitation is the name given to the set of procedures that are applied when a person is not breathing, and their heart has possibly stopped. The full set of procedures is known as cardiopulmonary resuscitation (CPR). *Cardio* relates to the heart and *pulmonary* to the lungs.

A person whose heart has stopped (cardiac arrest), or who is not breathing (respiratory arrest), needs immediate treatment to

ABC OF RESUSCITATION

Above
Lay the victim on his back, tilt the head back, and lift the chin to open the airway. Look at the victim's chest for signs of breathing.

Above
If the victim is not breathing, pinch the nose shut and keep the chin tilted. Seal your mouth over the victim's and give 2 breaths.

Above
Place interlocked hands on the victim's breastbone, press down, then release. Alternate 15 chest compressions with 2 rescue breaths.

WHAT CAN BLOCK THE AIRWAY?

The airway is made up of the nose, mouth, and windpipe (trachea). These carry air, containing oxygen, to the lungs and remove the waste product carbon dioxide from the lungs. If the airway becomes blocked, the oxygen levels in the body drop and eventually the vital organs such as the brain and heart stop working. Death will follow unless action is taken.

A number of things can block the airway: blood, food, and vomit are among the main culprits. In an unconscious person,

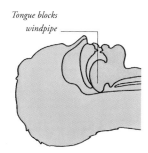

Tongue blocks windpipe

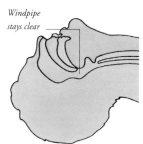

Windpipe stays clear

however, the biggest risk is from the tongue. When a person loses consciousness the muscles relax. If the person is lying on his back the tongue will fall to the back of the mouth, blocking off the windpipe and stopping oxygen getting into the body.

Clearing the airway is the first step of the essential ABC of first aid. The method of clearing an airway blocked by the tongue is very simple. By tilting the head back and lifting the chin, the tongue is prevented from falling to the back of the throat and the windpipe remains clear.

improve the chances of survival. Since speed is a key factor in survival, the treatment needs to be started before the arrival of the emergency ambulance and, since most cardiac arrests happen in the home or in the presence of a family member, friend, or colleague, CPR skills are essential for everyone to know.

The best outcomes from cardiac or respiratory arrest are achieved when all the steps in the Chain of Survival (see panel) are in place.

CHAIN OF SURVIVAL

- Early call for help
- Early CPR
- Early defibrillation
- Early medical care

The first two of these steps are often in the hands of the first aider.

AN EARLY CALL FOR HELP Ambulances today carry a range of equipment and treatments vital to the survival of seriously ill victims. Calling for an ambulance early is an essential part of the Chain of Survival, particularly for a victim whose heart has stopped.

EARLY CPR CPR works by putting oxygen into the blood through breathing into the victim's mouth or nose and by pushing the blood around the body by pressing on the chest and compressing the heart. The goal is to keep the person alive until emergency help arrives. Sometimes CPR alone will revive somebody whose heart has stopped but more often it is used to buy time until more advanced procedures are available.

EARLY DEFIBRILLATION The most effective treatment for an adult whose heart has stopped pumping blood is defibrillation. In simple terms, this is an electric shock delivered in a very specific way to encourage the heart to begin beating effectively again. Defibrillators are carried in most ambulances but are also increasingly found in public places such as shopping malls, railway stations, and airports, where local workers will have been trained in their use. Their early use is an essential factor in their effectiveness, highlighting again the need for an early call for help.

EARLY MEDICAL CARE Medical treatments following cardiac and respiratory arrest are improving all the time. Early access to such treatments in the ambulance and in hospital play a major role in long-term survival rates.

THE PRINCIPAL STEPS OF RESUSCITATION
These are detailed on the following pages:

- Check for danger to yourself and the victim.
- Check for a response from the victim.

If there is no response
- Open the airway.
- Check for breathing.

If there is no breathing
- Give 2 effective rescue breaths.
- Check for signs of circulation.

If there are no signs of circulation
- Start CPR.

CALLING FOR AN AMBULANCE

- Dial 911.
- Ask for the ambulance service.
- Listen to the operator—you will be asked for your name, contact details, and where you are.
- The operator will ask a series of questions about the victim and what has happened— give as much information as you can.
- Often the operator will give you advice on what to do next.
- Do not hang up the phone until you are told to do so.

WHEN TO CALL AN AMBULANCE

1 If you are alone, breathing is absent, and the victim is an adult, call for an ambulance and/or for access to a defibrillator as soon as you realise the victim is not breathing. The cause is most likely to be a heart attack leading to cardiac arrest, and the most effective treatment is CPR and very early access to defibrillation.

2 If you are alone and the victim is an infant or a child under 8 years of age, provide 1 minute of rescue breathing or full CPR before calling for an ambulance. The cause is most likely to be a problem with breathing, such as choking or drowning, etc., and the most effective treatment is to get oxygen into the lungs.

3 If you are not alone, send a bystander for the ambulance as soon as you have confirmed that the victim is not breathing.

Above
Call for an ambulance immediately if you are alone and the victim has stopped breathing. The person is likely to have had a heart attack and will need early defibrillation from trained personnel.

SOURCES OF MEDICAL HELP

- Ambulance
- Hospital Emergency Department
- Doctor's office
- Urgent case clinics
- Pharmacies

There is a variety of sources of medical assistance throughout the country. Investigate what is available locally before an emergency happens, and keep a list of useful numbers by the phone or stored in your cellular phone.

What to do when Somebody has Collapsed

Facing a situation where somebody has collapsed is frightening, particularly if it is somebody you know. However, there are some very simple steps that you can take to help you decide the best course of action, which in an emergency could mean the difference between life and death.

CHECK THE SCENE Is it safe for you to approach the person who has collapsed? Do not become a victim yourself. Check for dangers such as chemicals, electricity, or traffic. If you can safely remove the danger, do so. If not, consider if you can safely and easily move the person from the danger, or whether you need to call for additional help such as the fire service.

CHECK THE RESPONSE Is the person who has collapsed conscious?
● Gently squeeze the shoulders and ask loudly, "Are you all right?"
● Speak loudly and clearly.
● Always assume there may be a neck injury and squeeze gently.

Below
The most important rule of first aid is never to put yourself in danger. Do not rush to the scene; look around you to assess potential dangers. If in doubt, stay back.

For babies and young children

Do not squeeze the shoulders—try to provoke a response by stroking the cheek or the sole of the foot and speaking loudly.

IF THERE IS NO RESPONSE If there is no response, the immediate danger is that the victim might be unconscious and may have a blocked airway or be in need of resuscitation.

- Shout for help.
- If possible, leave the victim in the position in which you found him and open the airway.
- When it is not possible to carry out an assessment of the victim in the position found, turn him onto his back and open the airway.

OPEN THE AIRWAY

- Place one hand on the forehead and gently tilt the head back.
- Remove any obvious obstructions from the victim's mouth, including dislodged dentures, but leave well-fitting dentures in place.
- Place the fingertips of two fingers under the point of the victim's chin and lift the chin. If injury to the neck is suspected, handle the head very gently and try to avoid tilting the head too much.

For a baby, use only one finger to lift the chin and take particular care not to overtilt the head.

CHECK FOR BREATHING Once the airway is open, the next priority is to check whether or not the person is breathing. Keep the airway open with one hand on the forehead and one hand lifting the chin. Put your cheek to the victim's face and look down the chest.

- LOOK for the movement of the chest and stomach.
- LISTEN for breath sounds.
- FEEL for breathing on the side of your face.

If the victim is breathing, turn into the recovery position.

If the victim is not breathing

- Call 911 for emergency help.

If you have not already done so, make sure that an ambulance has been called.

- Start resuscitation.

ABC OF RESUSCITATION

Airway Ensure a clear airway.

Breathing Check breathing and provide rescue breathing to the non-breathing person.

Circulation Check that the person has a good circulation and help them if their circulation has stopped or is damaged.

The Recovery Position for Adults

An unconscious person is always at risk of the airway becoming blocked by the tongue. There is also the possibility of choking on stomach contents because the valve holding food down often relaxes, allowing food to come back up into the mouth. If there is damage to the mouth or internal injuries, a person may also be at risk of choking on blood. To try to reduce these risks, most unconscious people are safest if placed in the recovery position while waiting for help to arrive. This position keeps the airway open and allows liquids to drain from the mouth.

ASSESSING A VICTIM If somebody is unconscious (not responsive) but breathing, your priorities are: to ensure that she stays breathing by keeping the airway unblocked and regularly looking, listening, and feeling for breaths; to treat any life-threatening injuries such as serious bleeding; and to call for emergency help. For an unconscious person who you know to be breathing, do a quick check for life-threatening injuries such as severe bleeding and treat if necessary, then move the victim into the recovery position.

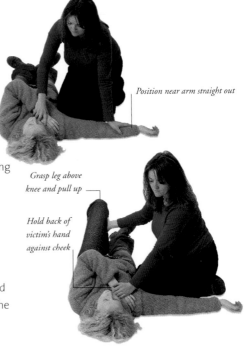

Position near arm straight out

Grasp leg above knee and pull up

Hold back of victim's hand against cheek

HOW TO MOVE AN ADULT INTO THE RECOVERY POSITION

1 Kneel beside the victim. Remove glasses and any bulky objects from the pockets. Ensure the airway is open by lifting the chin and tilting the head. Make sure both legs are straight, then place the arm nearest to you straight out from the victim's body, with the palm facing upward.

2 Bring the arm furthest away from you across the victim's chest and hold the back of the hand against the cheek nearest to you.

3 With your other hand, grasp the far leg just above the knee and pull it up, keeping the foot flat on the ground.

4 Keeping the victim's hand pressed against his or her cheek, pull on the far leg and roll the victim toward you and on to his or her side. Adjust the upper leg so that both the hip and knee are bent at right angles.

5 Tilt the head back so that the airway remains open. If necessary, adjust the hand under the cheek to make sure the victim's head remains tilted and the airway stays open. Call for emergency help if this has not already been done. Check the breathing regularly, and check the lower arm for any loss of color or warmth. If it turns white or blue, or if it gets cold, gently move it until the color or warmth returns.

Hip and knee bent at right angles

Tilt the head back so that the airway remains open

ABC OF FIRST AID	SPINAL INJURY

ABC OF FIRST AID

Airway Use the recovery position to help maintain an open airway.

Breathing Continue to check breathing while the person is in the recovery position.

Circulation Treat any life-threatening bleeding.

SPINAL INJURY

If the victim has been involved in an accident that involved a lot of force, such as a fall from a height or an automobile accident, the back or neck may be injured. The priority in an unconscious person will always be ABC. If you suspect a person may have a neck or back injury, or other broken bones, you may wish to adjust the recovery position to minimize movement. Gently move the head to a position where vomit or blood can drain out. If you are concerned about breathing, the person must be moved into a safer position. See warning about spinal injuries in children, page 22.

The Recovery Position for Children and Babies

The priorities for an unconscious child are to ensure that the child stays breathing by keeping the airway clear, and regularly looking, listening and feeling for breaths; to treat any life-threatening injuries; and to call for emergency help. If an unconscious child is breathing, do a quick check for life-threatening injuries and treat if necessary, then turn the victim into the recovery position.

HOW TO MOVE A CHILD INTO THE RECOVERY POSITION

1 Kneel beside the child. Remove glasses and any bulky objects from the pockets. Ensure the airway is open by lifting the chin and tilting the head. Make sure both legs are straight, then place the arm nearest to you straight out from the child's body, with the elbow bent and the palm facing upward.

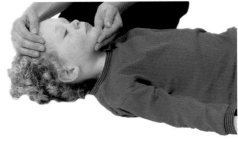

WARNING

Never move a child if you suspect there is a spinal injury unless breathing is hindered or the child needs to be removed from danger.

2 Bring the arm furthest away from you across the child's chest and hold the back of the hand against the cheek nearest to you.

Back of child's hand rests against cheek

3 With your other hand, grasp the child's far leg just above the knee and pull it up, keeping the foot flat on the ground.

Make sure hip and knee are bent at right angles

4 Keeping the child's hand pressed against her cheek, pull on the far leg and roll the child toward you and on to her side. Adjust the upper leg so that both the hip and knee are bent at right angles.

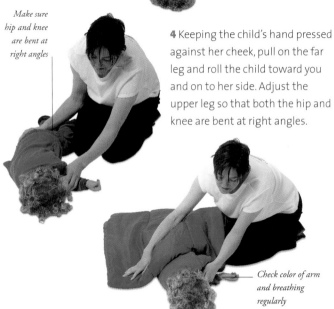

Check color of arm and breathing regularly

RECOVERY POSITION FOR BABIES

For a baby or a very young child who is unconscious, the easiest way to maintain an open airway is to cradle the infant face down over your arm, while supporting the head and neck with your hand.

5 Tilt the head back so that the airway remains open. If necessary, adjust the hand under the cheek to make sure the child's head remains tilted and the airway stays open. Call for emergency help if this has not already been done. Check the breathing regularly, and check the lower arm for any loss of color or warmth. If it turns white or blue, or if it becomes cold, gently move it until the color or warmth returns.

Rescue Breathing for Adults

When a person is not breathing the body suffers from shortage of oxygen, and if no action is taken this will eventually lead to death. The air that a healthy adult breathes out contains a valuable amount of oxygen, which can be shared with a person who is not breathing to help restore his or her oxygen levels. This process is often called mouth-to-mouth resuscitation or artificial respiration; the actual breaths are called rescue breaths.

RESCUE BREATHING Rescue breathing is provided to a person who is not breathing. When an adult is not breathing, the cause is very likely to be a problem with the heart. It is therefore essential that as soon as you realize that an adult is not breathing, you make sure that an ambulance has been called. If you have a face shield or mask and know how to use it, this can be valuable, but do not waste time looking for one.

In the case of face injury or if a person has been poisoned, provide mouth-to-nose rescue breathing. Lift the chin, tilt the head, seal the mouth, and breathe into the nose, removing your mouth to let air escape.

1 Place the victim on her back. Open the airway by tilting the head and lifting the chin with two fingers.

2 Pinch the soft part of the nose closed with the finger and thumb of the hand that was on the forehead. Open the mouth.

3 Take a deep breath to fill your lungs with air and place your lips around the victim's mouth, making sure you have a good seal.

Airway Use head tilt and chin lift to keep an open airway while providing rescue breathing.

Breathing Provide rescue breathing to somebody who is not breathing.

Circulation Check for signs of circulation.

4 Blow steadily into the mouth and watch the chest rise. Maintaining head tilt and chin lift, take your mouth away and watch the chest fall.

An effective breath is one where you see the chest rise and fall. Your goal is to give 2 effective breaths. Try up to 5 attempts to give 2 effective breaths.

CHECKING FOR CIRCULATION After giving 2 effective breaths, the next step in the ABC of first aid is to check that the oxygen is being circulated through the body. Look, listen, and feel for breathing, coughing, movement, normal color or any other sign of life for not more than 10 seconds. If there are clear signs of circulation, then continue to give rescue breaths at a rate of 1 every 6 seconds until help arrives or the person begins to breathe for himself. Continue to check for signs of circulation throughout.

   If there are no signs of circulation, you will need to move to giving the casualty full CPR—combining rescue breaths with chest compressions (see pages 29–30).

WHAT TO DO IF THE CHEST DOES NOT RISE

● Check for any obvious obstruction around the neck or on the chest which may be preventing the breath from going in.
● Re-open the airway. Tilt the head, look for and remove any obvious obstructions, and lift the chin.
● Re-seal the nose and mouth and breath in again.
● Try up to 5 more attempts to give 2 effective breaths.

If the chest still does not rise, it is likely that the airway is blocked either by an object such as food or vomit or because the air passages have swollen up due to a condition such as anaphylaxis (see pages 50–51). In these circumstances, the best treatment is to move straight to CPR, checking for circulation and combining further attempts at rescue breaths with chest compressions.

Rescue Breathing for Children and Babies

If a child has lost consciousness and is not breathing, you will need to provide rescue breathing in order to prevent brain damage and heart failure. When a child is not breathing, the cause is very likely to be a problem with the intake of oxygen, for example, through drowning, an accident, or through choking. The priority, therefore, is to provide oxygen. If you are by yourself and an ambulance has not yet been called, do not leave to call an ambulance until you have given a minute's worth of rescue breathing (or if the circulation has also stopped, a minute's worth of CPR, where rescue breathing is combined with chest compressions).

RESCUE BREATHING FOR A CHILD

1 Place the child on his back. Open the airway by tilting the head and lifting the chin up with your fingers.

2 Pinch the soft part of the nose closed with the finger and thumb of the hand that was on the forehead. Open the mouth.

3 Take a deep breath to fill your lungs with air and place your lips around the child's mouth, making sure you have a good seal.

4 Blow into the mouth and watch the chest rise. Maintaining head tilt and chin lift, remove your mouth and watch the chest fall.

RESCUE BREATHING FOR A BABY

1 Open the airway by lifting the chin. Use minimum head tilt.

2 You may find it easier to seal your mouth over the baby's mouth and nose rather than trying to pinch the nose separately. Open the infant's mouth. Empty your cheeks of air rather than blowing hard into the mouth. Watch the chest rise.

3 Keeping the baby's chin lifted, take your mouth away and watch the chest fall.

An effective breath is one where you see the chest rise and fall, and your aim is to give 2 effective breaths. Try up to 5 attempts to give 2 effective breaths.

WHAT TO DO IF THE CHEST DOES NOT RISE

● Check for any obvious obstruction around the neck or on the chest which may be preventing the breath from going in.
● Re-open the airway. Tilt the head, look for and remove any obvious obstructions, and lift the chin.

● Re-seal the nose and mouth and breathe in again.
● Try up to 5 attempts to give 2 effective breaths.

If the chest still does not rise, it is likely that the airway is blocked either by an object such as food or vomit, or because the air passages have swollen up due to a condition such as anaphylaxis (see pages 50–51). In these circumstances, the best treatment is to move straight to CPR—combining further attempts at rescue breathing with chest compressions.

ABC OF RESUSCITATION FOR CHILDREN

Airway Use head tilt and chin lift to keep an open airway while providing rescue breathing.

Breathing Provide rescue breathing to a child or baby who is not breathing.

Circulation Check for signs of circulation.

CHECKING FOR CIRCULATION After giving 2 effective breaths, the next step in the ABC of first aid is to check that oxygen is being circulated around the body. Look, listen, and feel for breathing, coughing, movement, normal color or any other sign of life for no more than 10 seconds. If there are clear signs of circulation, then continue to give rescue breaths at a rate of 1 every 6 seconds, until help arrives or the child begins to breathe for himself. Continue to check for signs of circulation throughout.

If there are no signs of circulation, move to giving full CPR—combining rescue breaths with chest compressions (see pages 31–33).

In the case of face injury or if a child has been poisoned, give mouth-to-nose rescue breaths. Lift the chin, tilt the head, seal the mouth, and breathe into the child's nose, removing your mouth to let air escape.

CPR for Adults

Cardiopulmonary resuscitation (CPR) combines rescue breathing with chest compressions to circulate oxygen around the body while waiting for further emergency help. CPR does not normally restart a person's heart but when it is combined with early emergency help, early defibrillation (whereby a brief electric shock is given to the heart), and early advanced hospital care, it has saved many lives. Ribs may be broken during CPR but this is preferable to dying.

GIVING CPR After providing the initial rescue breathing (see pages 24–25), you need to check the circulation to see if the heart is effectively pumping blood, and therefore oxygen, around the body. Look, listen, and feel for breathing, coughing, movement, normal color, or any other sign of life for not more than 10 seconds. If there are no signs of circulation, or you are at all unsure, start chest compressions. These must be given with the victim lying on his back on a firm surface.

ABC OF RESUSCITATION

Airway Use head tilt and chin lift to keep the airway open while providing rescue breathing.

Breathing Provide rescue breathing to somebody who is not breathing.

Circulation Check for signs of circulation and combine rescue breathing with chest compressions if you think the heart has stopped beating.

CHEST COMPRESSIONS

1 With your lower hand, locate one of the bottom ribs. Slide the fingers of one hand along the rib to the point where the rib meets the breastbone. Place one finger at this point and the finger next to it above it on the breastbone. Place the heel of your other hand on the breastbone and slide it down until it reaches your index finger. This is the point at which you should apply pressure.

2 Place the heel of your first hand on top of the other hand and interlock your fingers. Lean well over the victim and, with your arms straight, press down vertically and depress the breastbone one-third of the depth of the chest, which on an adult is 1½–2 inches.

3 Release the pressure without losing contact between your hands and the breastbone. Compress the chest 15 times, at a rate of 100 compressions per minute. Compression and release should take an equal amount of time.

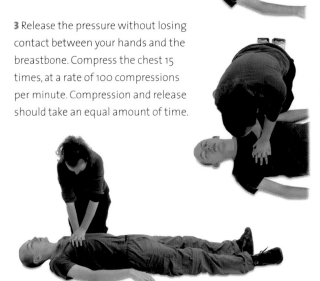

COMBINING CHEST COMPRESSIONS WITH RESCUE BREATHS Chest compressions circulate blood to the vital organs such as the brain. To ensure that this blood contains oxygen, you need to combine chest compressions with rescue breaths.

After 15 compressions, tilt the head, lift the chin, and give 2 effective breaths. Continue until:
● Emergency help arrives.
● The victim shows signs of circulation.
● You become so exhausted you cannot carry on.

IF THE VICTIM VOMITS

The combination of being unconscious with no muscle tone to hold in the stomach contents, air possibly being blown into the stomach through rescue breathing, and compressing the chest may result in the victim being sick. He or she will often have lost the reflex that causes gagging so the vomit may stay at the back of the throat or come into the mouth. This must be cleared promptly:

● Roll the person toward you, supporting the head.
● Open the mouth and sweep out any vomit with two fingers.
● Turn the person onto his back and start the ABC process again.

You may wish to use a face shield when providing rescue breathing, but not having one should not stop you performing CPR. You can also give breaths through a handkerchief.

CPR for Children and Babies

If a child or infant has no pulse and is not breathing you will need to give CPR

(cardiopulmonary respiration) to enable the body's vital organs to continue functioning.

After providing the initial rescue breathing, check the circulation to see if the heart is effectively

pumping blood, and therefore oxygen, around the body. Look, listen, and feel for breathing,

coughing, movement, normal color or any other sign of life for no more than 10 seconds.

If there are no signs of circulation, or if you are at all unsure, start chest compressions.

This must be given with the child lying on their back on a firm surface.

CHEST COMPRESSIONS FOR CHILDREN

These techniques broadly apply for a child between 1 and 7 years old. However, you should take into account the size of the child when deciding whether to use the techniques for children or infants.

1 Place the heel of one hand on the lower half of the breastbone. Lean well over the victim and, with your arm straight, press vertically down and depress the breastbone one-third of the depth of the chest.

2 Release the pressure without losing contact between your hands and the breastbone. Compress the chest 5 times at a rate of 100 compressions per minute. Compression and release should take an equal amount of time.

Press down the heel of your hand on the breastbone

COMBINING CHEST COMPRESSIONS WITH RESCUE BREATHING FOR CHILDREN

Chest compressions circulate blood to the vital organs such as the brain. To ensure that this blood contains oxygen, you need to combine chest compressions with rescue breathing. The procedure is the same as CPR for an adult but the chest compressions are not as forceful

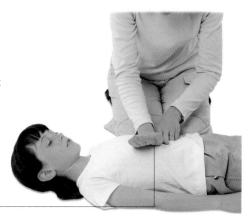

and the rate of breaths and compressions is different. After 5 compressions, tilt the head, lift the chin and give 1 effective breath. Continue this cycle of CPR. Do not interrupt the CPR sequence unless the child makes a movement or takes a breath on her own.

Continue until:
● Emergency help arrives and takes over.
● The child shows signs of circulation.
● You become so exhausted you cannot carry on. (Try to find someone to take over until medical help arrives.)

CHEST COMPRESSIONS FOR BABIES
These techniques broadly apply for a baby under 1 year. However, a large baby may require the techniques for a child and a small child may be better with the techniques for a baby.

1 Place the two fingers of one hand on the lower half of the breastbone. Lean well over the baby and, with your arm straight, press vertically down and depress the breastbone one-third of the depth of the chest.

2 Release the pressure without losing contact between your hands and the breastbone. Compress the chest 5 times at a rate of 100 compressions per minute. Compression and release should take an equal amount of time.

COMBINING CHEST COMPRESSIONS WITH RESCUE BREATHS FOR BABIES
Chest compressions circulate blood to the vital organs, and to ensure that this blood contains oxygen, chest compressions need to be combined with rescue breathing.

After 5 compressions, lift the baby's chin and give 1 effective breath. Continue this cycle of 5 compressions to 1 effective breath. Do not interrupt the CPR sequence unless the baby makes a movement or takes a breath on her own. Continue until:
● Emergency help arrives and takes over.
● The baby shows signs of circulation.
● Somebody can take over from you if you are exhausted.

Left
If the baby has no pulse and is not breathing you will have to give CPR. Lay her down on a firm surface and position two fingers in the middle of the chest.

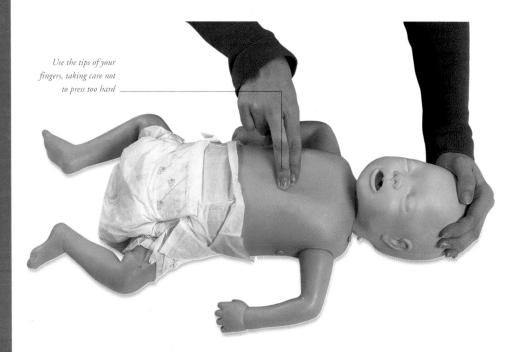

Use the tips of your fingers, taking care not to press too hard

WHEN TO CALL FOR HELP With children and babies, the heart is most likely to stop because of problems with breathing. Therefore, if you are alone and have to call for an ambulance yourself, you should give 1 minute of CPR before leaving to make the call. This will ensure that oxygen has been circulated around the body, the most effective treatment for breathing problems. If the child is small enough, you may be able to carry her to the phone with you. Try not to leave the child unattended. If the infant recovers at any time, stop performing CPR but monitor the breathing and circulation rates until medical help arrives.

ABC OF RESUSCITATION

Airway Use head tilt and chin lift to keep airway open while providing rescue breathing.

Breathing Provide rescue breathing to a baby who is not breathing.

Circulation Check for signs of circulation and combine rescue breathing with chest compressions if you think the heart has stopped beating.

Choking in Adults

Choking is a blockage in the windpipe that makes it difficult or impossible for a person to breathe because air cannot pass into the lungs. Somebody who is choking will often do so quietly, initially turning red as he or she struggles to take air in, grasping at the neck and mouth and eventually losing color, with a blue tinge to the lips. Without treatment, a person will become unconscious and will die. Choking in adults is often as a result of eating a meal too quickly or of eating on the move.

TREATMENT FOR AN ADULT WHO IS CHOKING

If the victim is able to speak or cough, then the situation is less serious. Encourage him or her to continue coughing if able. Check the mouth to see if any obstacle can be easily removed. Do not sweep in the mouth blindly, and take great care not to push down into the throat. If at any time the person shows signs of becoming weak, stops breathing or coughing, or begins to lose color and turn blue, perform the Heimlich maneuver immediately.

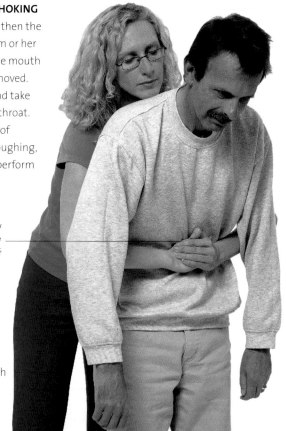

When someone is choking, prompt, calm action can save their life

THE HEIMLICH MANEUVER

The purpose of this maneuver is to displace any obstruction blocking the windpipe by forcing a cough. Stand or kneel behind the casualty and put both arms around the upper abdomen. Clench your fist and place it, thumb side in,

Left

Make a fist and position the thumb first in the middle of the victim's abdomen, just below the breastbone.

between the belly button and the bottom of the breastbone. Grasp it with your other hand. Keep your arms away from the ribcage and pull sharply inwards and upward 4 times. This movement thrusts the diaphragm up toward the lungs, creating a cough.

For a casualty who is lying down or unconscious, place the heel of one hand just below the breastbone. Place the other hand on top and give 4 short, upward thrusts.

Below

Place the heel of one hand just below the breastbone. Place the other hand on top.

If the obstruction is still not relieved, repeat the maneuver. Recheck the mouth for any object that can be reached with a finger and remove it if possible. Perform the maneuver 3 times, then call for emergency help.

WHAT IF THE PERSON BECOMES UNCONSCIOUS? Open the airway by tilting the head, checking the mouth, and lifting the chin. If the victim is breathing, falling unconscious might have freed the object sufficiently to allow air through. Turn the person into the recovery position (see pages 20–21), maintaining a careful check on breathing. If the victim is not breathing, provide rescue breathing (see pages 24–25) and move on to the normal CPR procedures (see pages 29–30).

If you know that the person has choked and the chest does not rise when rescue breathing is attempted, move straight to chest compressions without assessment of circulation. Check the mouth after every set of compressions. The chest compressions act as an artificial cough and may help expel the object from the windpipe. Make sure that you call for emergency help as soon as possible.

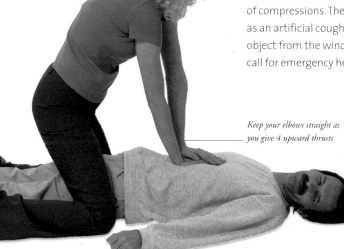

Keep your elbows straight as you give 4 upward thrusts

Choking in Children

Children often put small objects into their mouths which may cause choking. This is an obstruction in the windpipe that makes it difficult or impossible to breathe as air cannot pass into the lungs. A child who is choking will often do so quietly, initially turning red as he or she struggles to take air in, grasping at the neck and mouth and eventually losing color, with a blue tinge to the lips. Without treatment, a child will become unconscious and may die.

CHOKING IN CHILDREN Choking is a major cause of death in young children and should be considered whenever a child has breathing difficulties. Look for small beads or coins that the child may have been playing with, or ask playmates to identify clues that choking may be the cause of unconsciousness in the child.

TREATMENT Check a child's mouth for obstruction but do not feel blindly in the mouth as you may push the object further into the windpipe. Look to see if there is anything that can be easily removed. If the child is breathing, encourage her to continue coughing because this may dislodge the obstruction. If the child shows signs of becoming weak or stops breathing or coughing, perform the Heimlich Maneuver.

THE HEIMLICH MANEUVER
This maneuver works by producing an artificial cough that dislodges the object blocking the windpipe. Stand or kneel behind the child. Put your arms around her waist. Make a fist with one hand and place it, thumb side in, between the belly button and the bottom of the breastbone. Grasp the fist with your other hand. Keep your arms

Left
Carefully check the mouth for any object that can be reached with a finger.

away from the child's ribcage and give 4 sharp inward and upward thrusts. The aim is to relieve the obstruction with each thrust. It may be necessary to repeat this maneuver before the object is coughed up.

If the obstruction is still not relieved, recheck the mouth for any object that can be reached with a finger and remove it if possible. Perform the maneuver 3 times before calling for emergency help.

Keep your arms off the child's rib cage

Give 4 short thrusts inward and upward

Choking in Babies

Babies under one year are most likely to choke on their vomit. Look in the mouth. If you can easily remove the cause of the problem, then do so, but take great care not to touch the back of the throat or to push the object further in.

Perform the Heimlich maneuver on a baby by positioning it face down along your arm. Support the head with your hand. With the heel of your hand, give 4 sharp blows to the back. It may be necessary to repeat this procedure before the obstruction is cleared.

1 Position the baby so that the head is downward. Apply 4 sharp blows to the back with the heel of the hand. Check the mouth carefully for the object. You may need to repeat the cycle until the obstruction is coughed up.

If giving back slaps does not dislodge the object, you will need to perform chest thrusts.

Right
Rest your forearm on your leg and position the baby face downward (see step 1).

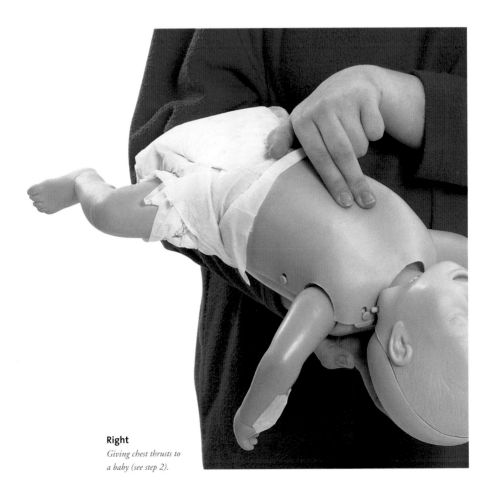

Right
*Giving chest thrusts to
a baby (see step 2).*

2 To give chest thrusts turn the baby over and place two fingers one finger width below the nipples. Give 4 sharp thrusts to a depth of 1 inch. It may be necessary to repeat until the object is coughed up.

Call for emergency help after repeating the cycle 3 times.

WHAT IF THE CHILD OR BABY BECOMES UNCONSCIOUS? Begin CPR (see pages 31–33). If the infant is not breathing and the chest does not rise when rescue breathing is attempted, move straight to chest compressions without assessment of circulation. Check the mouth after every set of compressions.

First Aid Procedures

Drowning

When a person is drowning, the air passages close to prevent water entering the lungs. This also prevents air from entering the lungs, thus depriving the victim of oxygen and eventually leading to unconsciousness and death. Usually, only if the victim has been unconscious in the water for some time do the lungs fill up with water. More commonly, the water goes into the stomach. A secondary risk for the rescued person is that he or she may choke on vomit as water in the stomach forces the stomach contents upward. A near-drowning person also faces the risk of hypothermia. Children and young adults are at the greatest risk of drowning.

RESCUING A DROWNING PERSON As in all first aid, the key rule is to protect yourself. A person who is drowning will strike out and pull down even the most competent swimmer; dirty water can hide dangers such as metal rubbish with sharp edges; and cold water can cause muscles to cramp very quickly.

If possible, reach to the person from the safety of solid ground using a pole, rope, or buoyancy aid to enable him to help himself out of the water. If in doubt about your ability to rescue the person safely, call for emergency help.

VOMITING A person who has nearly drowned is very likely to vomit. Maintain a close watch for this. If the victim vomits while you are resuscitating him, turn him toward you, and clear out the mouth before turning him on to the back and resuming rescue breathing. If the victim vomits while in the recovery position, clear out the mouth and keep a close eye on breathing to ensure that it has not stopped. If the victim is conscious and becomes sick,

Left
Make sure you are safe before attempting to rescue a drowning person; if in doubt call for emergency help. If possible, reach out to the person using a pole, a piece of rope, or buoyancy aid from the safety of solid ground.

TREATMENT OF A
NEAR-DROWNING VICTIM

Your priority is to ensure an open airway and that the person is breathing.

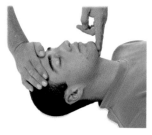

1 Open the airway by tilting the head, checking the mouth, and lifting the chin. Check for breathing for up to 10 seconds.

2 If the victim is breathing, place into the recovery position (see pages 20–21).

3 If the victim is not breathing, provide rescue breathing (see pages 24–28) before moving on to an assessment of circulation and full CPR (see pages 29–33) as necessary.

Cover with a warm blanket to reduce the risk of hypothermia

encourage him to lean forward and give support while he is vomiting.

Do not make any effort to remove water from the lungs by applying chest compressions or abdominal thrusts. The risk of water in the lungs is minimal, while compressing the chest or stomach will increase the risk of the victim choking on his own vomit.

HYPOTHERMIA Hypothermia is a lowering of the body's core temperature and is a very common secondary problem of near-drowning. If untreated, hypothermia leads to the breathing and heart rate slowing down and eventually stopping.

To reduce the risks of hypothermia in a case of near-drowning, place the victim on a blanket or layer of coats to insulate him from the ground. Remove wet clothing if you are able to replace it quickly with warm and dry clothing; if not, then cover the wet clothing with blankets and coats. Cover the head to prevent heat loss. Warm the external environment if possible.

Even in a conscious person, hypothermia can be a risk. Seek medical help as soon as possible. For further information on hypothermia, see pages 136–137.

Shock

The word shock can be used in a range of ways, but when used in a first aid context it describes a physical condition that results from a loss of circulating body fluid. It should not be confused with emotional shock that might occur when a person has received bad news (although the external signs are very similar).

WHAT HAPPENS IN CASES OF SHOCK A severe loss of body fluid will lead to a drop in blood pressure. Eventually the blood's circulation through the body will deteriorate and the remaining blood flow will be directed to the vital organs such as the brain. Blood will therefore be directed away from the outer areas of the body, so the victim will appear pale and the skin will feel cold and clammy. As blood flow slows, so does the amount of oxygen reaching the brain. The victim may appear to be confused, weak, and dizzy, and may eventually deteriorate into unconsciousness. To try to compensate for this lack of oxygen, the heart and breathing rates both speed up, gradually becoming weaker, and may eventually cease.

Potential causes of shock include: severe internal or external bleeding; burns; severe vomiting and diarrhea, especially in children and the elderly; problems with the heart.

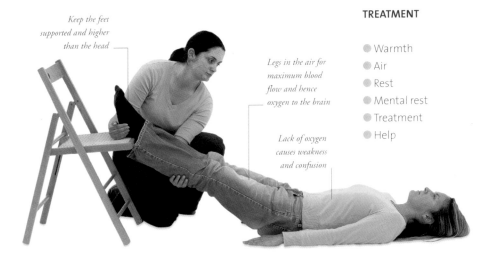

Keep the feet supported and higher than the head

Legs in the air for maximum blood flow and hence oxygen to the brain

Lack of oxygen causes weakness and confusion

TREATMENT

- Warmth
- Air
- Rest
- Mental rest
- Treatment
- Help

SIGNS AND SYMPTOMS

- Pale, cold, and clammy skin
- Fast, weak pulse
- Fast, shallow breathing
- Dizziness and weakness
- Confusion
- Unconsciousness
- Breathing and heartbeat stopping

Shock kills, so it is vital that you can recognize these signs and symptoms. With internal bleeding in particular, shock can occur some time after an accident, so if a person with a history of injury starts to display these symptoms coupled with any of the symptoms of internal bleeding (see pages 82–83), advise her to seek urgent medical attention, or take or send her to hospital.

Keep the patient warm to maintain blood flow and circulation

to allow maximum air to the victim.

Warmth Keep the victim warm but do not allow her to get overheated. If you are outside, try to get something underneath her if you can do so easily. Wrap blankets and coats around her, paying particular attention to the head, through which much body heat is lost.

Air Maintain a careful eye on the victim's airway and be prepared to turn her into the recovery position (see pages 20–23) if necessary, or even to resuscitate if breathing stops (see pages 24–28). Try to keep back bystanders and loosen tight clothing

Rest Keep the victim still and preferably sitting or lying down. If the victim is very giddy, lay her down with her legs raised to ensure that maximum blood and therefore maximum oxygen is sent to the brain.

Mental rest Reassure the victim but keep your comments realistic. Do not say that everything is going to be fine when it is obvious that there is something seriously wrong. Let the victim know that everything that can be done is being done and that help has been called for. If she has other concerns, try to resolve these.

Treatment Treat the cause of the shock and aim to prevent further fluid loss.

Help Ensure that appropriate medical help is on the way.

Breathing Difficulties

In a first aid situation you are likely to encounter a victim who has breathing difficulties.

Psychological stress may trigger breathing problems that affect the blood's chemical composition,

causing a range of symptoms that make the victim feel unwell. Accidents that include a heavy

impact to the chest can cause injuries that result in severe breathing difficulties.

HYPERVENTILATION This is a breathing difficulty that may be triggered by the stress of an accident or some other form of emotional shock. The person over-breathes, causing the level of carbon dioxide in the blood to drop. This leads to a combination of the signs and symptoms listed below:

- Fast, shallow breathing
- Feeling of tingling in the limbs
- Dizziness
- Cramps
- Panic attacks

Right

Reduced carbon dioxide levels in the blood can be restored to normal by slowly breathing into and out of a paper bag about 10 times and then breathing normally for 15 seconds until the rapid breathing ceases.

TREATMENT

1 If the victim is otherwise uninjured, remove her from the scene of the accident to a quiet place where there is no audience. People who are hyperventilating often subconsciously react to onlookers, making themselves worse.

2 Reassure the victim but remain calm and speak firmly. Encourage the victim to regain control of her breathing.

3 If the situation persists, and you are certain that there is no other underlying condition such as asthma or chest injury, let the victim inhale her own breathed-out air from a paper bag. This air contains more carbon dioxide, which will help restore the balance of oxygen and carbon dioxide in the blood.

4 Call a doctor or ambulance if symptoms do not disappear. Do not slap the victim—she may become violent and attack you, and you run the risk of being charged with assault.

CHEST INJURIES Serious injuries following an accident, or the aftermath of any illnesses causing problems with breathing, can lead to the lung collapsing. Air enters the space between the lung and the chest wall, making breathing very difficult. In severe cases, the pressure affects the uninjured lung and the heart, causing a tension pneumothorax, a condition requiring urgent medical attention if the victim is to survive.

Chest injuries with more than one broken rib will often result in the victim having difficulty in breathing as the chest wall is unable to move effectively. There may also be an open break on the chest wall where ribs have sprung out. Remember that the ribs extend around the back and there may be injuries here as well as on the front. See also Fractures of the Ribcage, pages 106–107.

Chest injuries may be accompanied by a sucking wound to the chest (see pages 106–107). Here there is a direct passage between the outside and the lungs, often caused by a puncture injury from a sharp object pushing through the chest wall.

SIGNS AND SYMPTOMS OF COLLAPSED LUNG AND OTHER CHEST INJURIES

- History of chest impact or recent illness affecting breathing
- Chest rises as the person breathes out (paradoxical breathing)
- Swelling or indentation along the line of the ribs
- Open fractures
- Difficulty in breathing
- Pain on breathing
- Shock, as there is likely to be some degree of internal bleeding (see pages 82–83)
- Bright red, frothy blood coming from the mouth and/or nose. (This is an indication of a punctured lung because oxygenated blood is escaping from the respiratory system. There may or may not be an associated sucking wound to the chest.)
- Sucking wound to the chest

TREATMENT Ensure that an early call for emergency medical help has been made. If the victim is conscious, she will often find it easier to breathe if sitting up. Help her into a sitting-up position if possible and provide support to remain in this position comfortably. If you can determine the side of the injury, lean the victim to the injured side. This helps relieve pressure on the good lung, allowing the victim to breathe a little easier.

If there is an open sucking wound to the chest, cover this up as soon as possible. The best cover comes from using plastic sealed on three sides over the wound area. Help the victim remove blood from her mouth. If the person becomes unconscious, place into the recovery position (see pages 20–23) on the injured side and monitor breathing carefully. Treat any open wound (see pages 69–70) once the person is in the recovery position. Treat any broken ribs (see pages 106–107).

Asthma

Asthma attacks cause the muscles of the air passages to go into spasm, making it very difficult for the asthmatic to breathe, particularly to exhale. Attacks may be triggered by an allergy or by stress; for example, being involved in an accident. Sometimes the cause of the attacks for a particular sufferer is never identified. There is evidence to suggest that asthma appears to be increasing in frequency, or at least in diagnosis.

TREATMENT

An asthma attack should not be underestimated. While the preventive treatments are very effective, and the drugs to relieve attacks usually work very well, left untreated, a serious attack can be fatal. The strain of a serious asthma attack can cause the breathing to stop or the heart to cease beating. You should be prepared to resuscitate (see pages 29–33) if necessary.

Helping an asthmatic stay calm is important

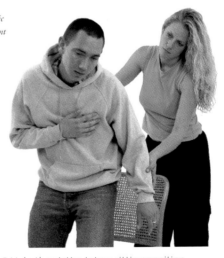

1 Reassure the victim as this will have a positive effect on his breathing.

2 Help the victim into a sitting position, leaning slightly forward, as most people with asthma find this an easier position for breathing.

Metered-dose inhaler delivers precise dose of drugs to relieve attack

3 If the victim has medication, enable him to use it. Inhalers are the main form of treatment.

If this is the first attack, the medication does not work within 5 minutes, or the victim is in severe distress, then call an ambulance. Help the victim to take medication every 5 to 10 minutes.

If the attack eases and the person finds it easier to breathe, he will not need immediate medical attention but should advise a doctor of the attack. A person will often be very tired following an attack so it is best to ensure that he is accompanied home to rest.

SIGNS AND SYMPTOMS

- History of the condition (although some people may not realize that they are asthmatic and the first attack may be a very severe one)
- Difficulty in breathing, particularly breathing out
- Wheezing or otherwise noisy breathing
- Inability to speak
- Pale skin and potential blueness, particularly around the lips, caused by lack of oxygen
- Distress, dizziness, and confusion as it becomes harder to get oxygen into the body
- Unconsciousness and then breathing stopping

USING AN INHALER

Known asthmatics are usually prescribed an inhaler, a device that administers a measured dose of drugs inhaled directly into the lungs, where it will have a near-instant effect.

Young children may find it hard to use an ordinary aerosol inhaler and will need a spacer instead. Medication is put into the end of the spacer and the child breathes normally to take this in.

Children under the age of four will usually require a face mask to use with the spacer as they cannot coordinate their breathing to inhale the drugs.

If a member of your family is an asthmatic, make sure that everyone understands the importance of knowing where the inhaler is and that there is always enough medication in the house.

Anaphylactic Shock

An allergy is hypersensitivity to a substance (allergen) that is not normally considered to be harmful. Allergies are triggered by the immune system, which reacts to the allergen as though it were a harmful substance invading the body. The most extreme response is anaphylaxis, which may result in anaphylactic shock which, if untreated, can kill.

CAUSES OF ANAPHYLAXIS This extreme allergic reaction has an intense effect on the body, causing a sudden drop in blood pressure and narrowing of the airways that can be fatal. Anaphylactic shock can be caused by anything, but among the most common triggers are: nuts (for those who are particularly sensitive, even touching the trace of a nut can be potentially fatal), seafood, insect stings and bites, and drugs (some people have a very extreme reaction to penicillin, for example).

As with asthma, the number of people suffering allergic reactions appears to be increasing. Whether this is because people are becoming more sensitive to allergens (the substances that cause allergic reactions) or whether we are just becoming better at detecting allergies, nobody is really sure.

SIGNS AND SYMPTOMS

One of the main effects of severe anaphylaxis is a constriction of the air passages in a similar way to asthma (see pages 48–49) but generally more severe, preventing the intake of any oxygen at all. There may be a history of contact with a particular allergen, the thing that triggers the attack. Anaphylaxis can happen very quickly, within seconds.

Signs and symptoms include:

- Difficulty breathing
- Pale skin and blue lips
- Blotches on the skin
- Rapid pulse
- Breathing and heartbeat stopping

Place the victim in the recovery position

Monitor airway, breathing, and circulation

TREATMENT

1 Call an ambulance immediately. The victim needs epinephrine to counteract the reaction.

2 If the victim is a known sufferer she may have an epinephrine injection. Help her to administer this. If you have been trained and the victim is unable to do so, you may give the injection.

3 Place the victim in the most comfortable position and reassure her.

4 If the victim becomes unconscious, place in the recovery position (see pages 20–23). Monitor the victim's breathing and circulation and be prepared to resuscitate if necessary (see pages 29–33).

Sit the victim in a comfortable position and reassure her

SKIN PRICK TEST FOR ALLERGIES

Skin prick tests are simple procedures carried out to find out what substances (allergens) cause allergic reactions in an affected person. Extracts of allergens that commonly cause allergic reactions, such as food, pollen, and dust are made into dilute solutions and are then placed on the skin. The skin is pierced to allow the substance to be absorbed.

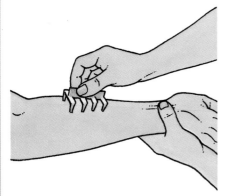

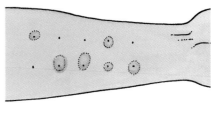

1 Dilute solutions of substances that a person is thought to be allergic to are placed on the skin, usually the arm, and the skin is then pricked with a needle. Several different allergens can be tested on the skin at the same time.

2 An allergic reaction usually takes place within 30 minutes of the test. If the person is allergic to the substance a red weal, indicating a positive reaction, appears at the site where the needle pricked the skin.

HANDLING AN ATTACK

Many anaphylaxis sufferers carry an auto-injector with a measured dose of a known treatment for an attack, most commonly epinaphrine. This will often look like a pen. It is easily administered by placing against the skin and clicking the end. Help the person having the attack to find and inject the medication.

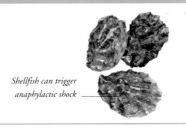

Shellfish can trigger anaphylactic shock

Heart Problems

The heart is a muscle that pumps blood around the body, which it does with the help of the thick-walled and muscular arteries and the other vessels of the circulatory system. The heart is controlled by regular electrical impulses that tell it when to contract. Like all other muscles, the heart needs its own blood supply and this is provided by the coronary (heart) arteries. When this blood supply fails to run smoothly, the body starts to experience problems, such as angina pectoris (angina) and heart attack. Either of these may lead to the heart stopping (cardiac arrest).

ANGINA Throughout life, arteries are clogging up with fatty deposits. As these fatty deposits cause the coronary and other arteries to become narrower, it becomes increasingly difficult for blood to flow around the body. The clogged coronary arteries can just about supply blood to the heart when it is pumping at a normal rate but when the heart rate speeds up the arteries cannot cope with the demand. This leads to an angina attack, a frightening, severe, crushing chest pain that acts as a warning to the victim to calm down or to rest.

TREATMENT

1 Sit the victim down and reassure her. This reduces the demands being placed on the heart.

2 Angina sufferers may have medicine that will help relieve an attack. This is often in the form of a puffer or a pill that is placed under the tongue. The drug works by dilating the blood vessels, thereby increasing circulation to the heart. Help the victim to take this medication.

3 Call an ambulance if the pain does not appear to ease or if the victim is not a known angina sufferer.

4 If the victim has regular attacks, listen to what she wants to do next.

SIGNS AND SYMPTOMS OF ANGINA

- Evidence of recent exertion
- Previous history of angina attacks
- Gripping chest pain, often described by the sufferer as vise-like
- Pain spreading up into the jaw or down into the left arm
- Feeling of tingling down the arm
- Shortness of breath
- Dizziness and confusion
- Anxiety
- Pale skin with possible blue tinges
- Rapid, weak pulse

HEART ATTACK If a coronary artery becomes completely blocked, the area of the heart being supplied by that particular blood vessel will be starved of oxygen and will eventually die. This blockage may be caused by a clot, a condition often referred to as a coronary thrombosis.

The development of advanced cardiac care in hospital and good post-hospital care means that heart attack patients have a good chance of making a full recovery. This is important information to remember when you are reassuring somebody having a heart attack.

SIGNS AND SYMPTOMS OF A HEART ATTACK

These signs and symptoms are generally the same as those of angina—indeed, the patient may initially suffer an angina attack that becomes a heart attack. The key difference is that heart attacks do not always follow physical exertion. While angina sufferers will recover from their attack on resting, heart attack patients do not tend to improve without medical treatment.

TREATMENT

1 Move the victim into a semi-sitting position, head and shoulders supported and knees bent, as this is generally the best position to breathe in.

Support shoulders and head to facilitate breathing

Keep knees bent and supported

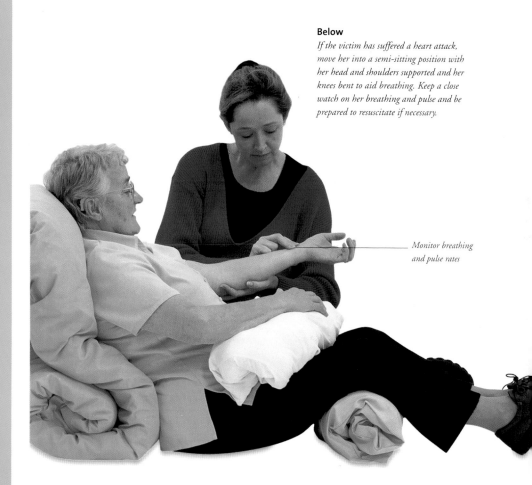

Below

If the victim has suffered a heart attack, move her into a semi-sitting position with her head and shoulders supported and her knees bent to aid breathing. Keep a close watch on her breathing and pulse and be prepared to resuscitate if necessary.

Monitor breathing and pulse rates

2 Reassure the victim and do not let her move, as this will place an extra strain on the heart.

3 Call for an ambulance as soon as possible because the victim needs hospital care.

4 If the victim has angina medication, let her take this. If you have an ordinary aspirin, give her one to chew (without water).

5 Keep a continual check on the breathing and pulse and be prepared to resuscitate if necessary (see pages 30–33).

Stroke

A stroke occurs when a blood clot or bleeding cuts off the blood supply, and therefore the oxygen, to part of the brain. The affected area of the brain will eventually die. The effect of a stroke depends on how much of the brain is affected and where the clot or bleeding is. Different parts of the brain control different functions, so a clot in the part of the brain that controls speech, for example, will result in slurred or confused speech. Often the signs will be confined to one side of the body.

EFFECTS OF STROKE If the bleeding or clot is in one of the larger blood vessels supplying a large area of the brain, then the stroke will often be immediately fatal. However, many people do survive, with some making a full recovery. Others may need extensive periods of rehabilitation and support to manage stroke-related problems such as reduced mobility.

TREATMENT Monitor airway and breathing and be prepared to resuscitate if necessary (see pages 24–28). Place the person in the recovery position if she becomes unconscious (see pages 20–23). If she is conscious, help her to lie down with the head and shoulders slightly raised. Provide support and reassurance. The person will often be

Below
If a person has had a stroke and is still conscious, help her to lie down with her head and shoulders raised. Speak in a reassuring voice and seek medical help.

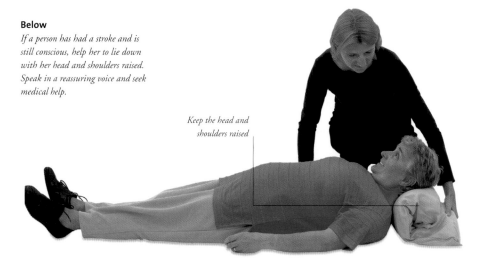

Keep the head and shoulders raised

Ask the person to smile to check for minor paralysis

Stretch arms out to check for loss of sensation or damage

Stroke may cause drooping or shaking

Left
Simple tests can be performed at home to assess whether or not a person has suffered a minor stroke. A minor stroke may cause weakness on one side of the body or a loss of sensation.

SIGNS AND SYMPTOMS

Any combination of the following may be present. In minor strokes, the signs and symptoms may be very limited.

● History—the sufferer may have a history of smaller strokes over previous years, or may have been feeling unwell for some days with no known cause
● Headache
● Blurred vision, partial loss of sight, or seeing flashing lights
● Confusion and disorientation, often mistaken for drunkenness
● Signs of paralysis or weakness, often only down one side of the body (confirm by asking the patient to hold out both arms in front of her and look for drooping or shaking)
● Difficulty speaking; drooping mouth or smile (caused by minor paralysis)
● Dribbling from one side of the mouth
● Loss of consciousness (this can be gradual or sudden)
● Sometimes the pulse will be full and throbbing, the person's breathing noisy, and the skin flushed

disorientated and may be speaking nonsense if the speech center is affected. Equally, she may hear what you are saying but not understand it. Speak in a reassuring tone with confidence. Call an ambulance. Wipe any dribbling away from the side of the face and be prepared for the person to vomit.

Epilepsy

Epilepsy is a very common condition, best described as a rogue electrical discharge across the brain. As the body's functions are controlled by electrical impulses this discharge can lead to a number of physical reactions. Many things may start a seizure (fit): tiredness, stress, or flashing lights are common triggers.

MAJOR SEIZURE

This is what most people would recognize as epilepsy, and there are typically four stages:

1 Many people get a sense that a seizure is likely to occur.

2 The electrical impulses lead to a contraction in the muscles that causes the epilepsy sufferer to fall to the ground with a cry. This is known as the tonic phase. The victim's muscles may then go into spasm. This is known as the clonic stage. During this stage the victim will not be breathing.

3 When the convulsion is over, the victim will be in a state of unconsciousness.

4 On recovery from unconsciousness, the victim will be very sleepy and will want to rest for some time.

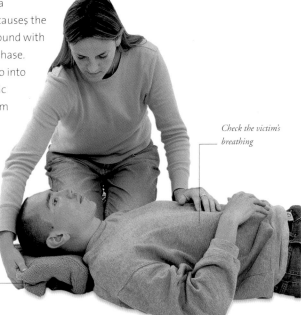

Check the victim's breathing

Right
Try to protect a person during an epileptic seizure by moving sharp or heavy objects out of the way and placing a pillow or folded article of clothing under the head to cushion it.

Protect the head by placing an article of clothing under it

MINOR FITS During a minor fit, somebody with epilepsy suffers a brief disturbance in the brain's normal activity, leading to a lack of awareness of his or her surroundings. To the observer it might seem like the person is daydreaming or has suddenly switched off.

There is little for you to do other than to guide the person away from danger and reassure him when he returns to normal. If he is not aware of any similar episodes happening before, advise him to see a doctor.

TREATMENT FOR A MAJOR EPILEPTIC SEIZURE

1 During the seizure, do not try to restrain the person. The muscular contractions are so strong during a fit that holding a person down may lead to broken bones—yours and his. Do not attempt to put anything in the mouth. Try to protect the victim—move sharp objects out of the way, remove constrictions and, if possible, place a soft coat under the head.

2 Once the seizure has finished, check the victim's airway and breathing and be prepared to resuscitate in the unlikely event that this is necessary (see pages 29–33). Place the person in the recovery position (see pages 20–23).

3 When the victim comes round, offer reassurance. The person may have lost control of bowel or bladder function so cover him up and, when he

Above
During a minor fit a person may appear to have suddenly switched off. If this happens, stay by the person so that you can reassure him when his behavior returns to normal. Seek medical advice if this is the first episode.

is steady on his feet, help him to find somewhere to clean up. He is likely to be very tired so, if possible, find him somewhere to lie down and sleep. Most of all, ask him what he wants to do—most epileptics manage the condition very well and will have their own coping strategies.

Left
After the seizure is over, check airway and breathing and place the victim in the recovery position.

INFANTILE CONVULSIONS (CAUSED BY HEAT)
Babies and young children may have seizures induced by a high temperature. This may be the result of an infection or because they are overwrapped and in a warm environment. The signs and symptoms are similar to a major epileptic seizure.

TREATMENT Make sure that the child is protected from hitting himself on a bed or cot—do not attempt to restrain. Cool down by removing bedclothes and clothing where possible. Sponge the head and under the arms with a tepid flannel or sponge, re-soaking it regularly. When the convulsion is finished, check ABC and take action as appropriate (see pages 12–13). In most cases, the child will want to sleep. Dress him in dry clothes and let him sleep. Call a doctor for advice.

WHEN TO CALL AN AMBULANCE Generally, neither epilepsy nor infantile convulsion are medical emergencies. However, you should be prepared to call an ambulance if:

- The victim is injured during the seizure.
- The seizure lasts for longer than 3 minutes.
- There are repeated seizures in a short period of time.
- The victim does not regain consciousness.

If it is the first seizure, advise the victim to call his doctor or take him to hospital.

Sponge the head with a tepid flannel or sponge to lower temperature

Protective bumper

Unconsciousness

Unconsciousness is an interruption of normal brain activity. It can happen suddenly or gradually. Unconsciousness can be caused by a range of injuries and medical conditions, as well as by a number of different drugs. An unconscious person may still have some reactions to pain or to commands, or may have no reactions at all.

Whatever the cause or degree of unconsciousness, the immediate emergency treatment remains the same:

● Assess whether the person is unconscious by gently squeezing the shoulders and asking a question.
● Open the airway by lifting the chin, clearing the mouth, and tilting the head.
● Check the breathing and be prepared to resuscitate if necessary (see pages 12–13).
● If breathing, check for life-threatening conditions and then turn into the recovery position (see pages 20-23).
● Call for emergency help.

This may be all that you have time to do before emergency help arrives. However, if you have longer, there are some things that you can do to gather information that may help medical staff with their diagnosis and treatment.

ASSESS THE LEVEL OF RESPONSE There is an agreed scale for assessing how responsive an injured or ill person is—the Glasgow Coma Scale. A fully alert person will score 15 while somebody who is totally unresponsive will score 3 with several variations in between (see observation chart, pages 238–239). You can help collect information to inform medical staff using some of the checks from this scale:

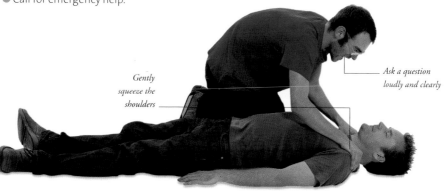

Gently squeeze the shoulders

Ask a question loudly and clearly

EYES Do they:
- Open without you having to ask the person to open them?
- Open on command?
- Open if you cause the person pain (this is often done by pinching the earlobe)?
- Remain closed?

MOVEMENTS Does the person:
- Understand and follow sensible instructions?
- Move only in response to pain?
- Not move at all?

SPEECH Does the person:
- Answer questions sensibly?
- Answer questions in a confused way?
- Make sounds that cannot be understood?
- Make no noise?

Do the checks of eyes, movement, and speech every 10 minutes and record your answers.

FAINTING

A faint is a brief loss of consciousness. Shock is one of the potential causes of fainting but other causes include lack of food, a reaction to emotional news, or long periods of inactivity, for example, guardsmen standing for a long time in the summer.

To treat someone who has fainted, open the airway and check for breathing (see pages 12–13). If the person is breathing and there are no signs of injury, then the best treatment is to lie her on her back with her legs raised. This puts maximum oxygen back to the brain and speeds up recovery from a faint. If she has not begun to come around after 3 minutes, or if breathing becomes difficult, put her into the recovery position and call for help.

Above
The easiest way to find the pulse is to press the hollow between the windpipe and large neck muscle with two fingers.

Above
A pulse can be found at the wrist, although this can be more difficult to locate.

EXAMINING THE UNCONSCIOUS PERSON

Your initial check of the injured or ill person will be for life-threatening conditions, particularly serious bleeding (see pages 66–68). If you have more time while waiting for the ambulance, a more thorough check may show up less serious injuries or illness and potential clues to the cause of unconsciousness. This check should never be at the cost of monitoring and maintaining the airway or of keeping the injured person as still as possible. If doing a check of the body, it is sensible to do so in the presence of a third person.

Check the body from head to toe, looking for areas of bleeding, signs of broken bones or burns, or clues as to the cause of unconsciousness.

Potential causes of unconsciousness and some clues to diagnosis

Cause	Clues
Hypoglycemia (low blood sugar)	Medic alert or card declaring diabetes, diabetic medication.
Epileptic fit	Medic alert or card declaring epilepsy. Medication.
Head injury	Blood, spinal fluid from ear or nose, dent or bump on the head, uneven pupils.
Stroke	Paralysis on one side of the body (may be apparent in somebody with a higher level of consciousness); uneven pupils.
Heart attack	Details from bystanders (e.g. collapsed holding his chest), pale skin, and blue lips.
Poisoning or drugs	Evidence of drugs or poisons, e.g. medicine bottles, syringes, empty canister with poisons label, etc. Abnormal heart and/or breathing rate/rhythm.
Fainting	Slipped rather than fell, pale before falling. May have epileptic-type movements afterwards.

MONITOR AND RECORD BREATHING

Breathing is measured by counting the number of breaths in 1 minute (one breath being one rise and fall of the chest).

MONITOR AND RECORD PULSE RATE

Pulse rate is measured by counting the number of beats at the pulse at either the neck or the wrist for 1 minute. The easiest place to feel a pulse is in the carotid artery in the neck, though you can also check the wrist. Take recordings of breathing and pulse rate every 10 minutes and write down the results for the medical staff.

Diabetes

Diabetes mellitus is a medical condition in which the body is unable to effectively regulate the amount of sugar in the blood. The pancreas (an organ in the body) normally produces a hormone called insulin that regulates blood sugar level. In a person suffering from diabetes this does not happen effectively and as a result blood sugar levels become too high (this is known as hyperglycemia). Most diabetics control the condition through a combination of diet and injections of insulin. Too much insulin can lead to a condition known as hypoglycemia (low blood sugar).

SIGNS AND SYMPTOMS

Early signs:
- Wanting to drink a lot (the body is trying to flush sugar from the system)
- Passing water regularly (urine may smell sweet)
- Lethargy

As the condition deteriorates:
- Dry skin and rapid pulse
- Deep, labored breathing
- Increasing drowsiness
- Breath or skin smells strongly of acetone (like nail-polish remover) as the body tries to get rid of sugar

HYPERGLYCEMIA Hyperglycemia is most likely to occur in an undiagnosed diabetic. Diabetes is generally first noticed in early adolescence or in middle age. If left untreated, a high blood sugar level will lead to unconsciousness and death. Onset may be gradual with deterioration often happening over a number of days.

TREATMENT During the early stages, encourage immediate contact with the local doctor. If this is difficult, or the condition deteriorates, take or send the person to hospital. Monitor airway and breathing and be prepared to resuscitate (see pages 29–33) if necessary.

HYPOGLYCAEMIA Low blood sugar level has a quick and serious effect on the brain. Most commonly it is caused by somebody with diabetes either taking too much insulin, or

SIGNS AND SYMPTOMS

● History of diabetes (however, a diabetic suffering a hypoglycemia attack is often confused or aggressive and may not admit to having diabetes)

● Hunger

● Feeling faint or dizzy

● Strange behavior: confusion, aggression, or even violence

● Pale, cold, sweaty skin

● Rapid loss of consciousness

● Shallow breathing

● Evidence of diabetes, e.g. medic alert, sugar solution, or syringe in pocket

● Evidence of recent heavy exercise or drinking

CONFUSION WITH OTHER CONDITIONS

It is not unusual for diabetes to be mistaken for other common situations such as drunkenness, substance abuse, compression (see Fractures of the Skull, Face, and Jaw, pages 96–97), or a stroke. The treatment in all these situations is to monitor and maintain the airway, be prepared to resuscitate if necessary, use the recovery position if the person becomes unconscious, and seek medical advice or call emergency help.

Do not make assumptions as to the cause of the problem. Instead, look for clues to diagnosis for the medical staff. Somebody who is drunk may also be suffering from head injury; the syringe in a person's coat may be for diabetic medication or for drug abuse. While you do not need to know the cause the medical staff do and any clues that you can hand over could be potentially life-saving.

taking the right amount of insulin and then either not eating enough or burning off sugar through vigorous exercise. Less commonly, it can accompany heat exhaustion, alcohol abuse, or epileptic fits.

TREATMENT If the person is unconscious, monitor the airway and breathing and be prepared to resuscitate as necessary.
If the person is fully conscious, help him to sit down or to lie down with the shoulders raised. Give something high in sugar and easy to consume, such as chocolate or a sugary drink, to try to restore the body's chemical balance.

If this marks an improvement, give more. If the condition does not improve, seek medical advice. Stay with the person until he recovers. Ask his guidance on what he wants to do next. Arrange for some help to take him home or to the doctor. If the condition continues to deteriorate, call an ambulance.

Bleeding

Blood is carried around the body in a transport system of arteries, capillaries, and veins, and any damage to this network results in bleeding. Bleeding can be both external and internal. External bleeding involves a break to the skin surface, known as a wound, which can take many different forms. Internal bleeding is bleeding that occurs inside the body when there is no external injury for the blood to escape from. The most common form of internal bleeding is a small bruise from a minor impact. Heavy impact from car accidents, fights, or falls, for example, can lead to serious internal bleeding, which may kill.

TRANSPORT OF BLOOD Arteries have thick muscular walls, that contract. This pushes blood out from the heart under pressure. The blood contained within them is full of oxygen, which has been collected from the lungs, and the main function of the arteries is to take this oxygen-rich blood to the organs and body tissue. Because the blood is under pressure, and is so full of oxygen, arterial bleeding is characterized by bright red blood pumping from an injury. Arterial bleeding is very serious as blood is rapidly lost.

Veins have thin walls and return blood from the organs and tissues to the heart. They do not have muscles of their own and rely on the actions of the muscles around them to squeeze the blood around. To keep the blood moving in one direction around the body, they have a series of one-way valves that ensure a one-way flow. When these valves deteriorate, blood pools in the veins, making them swell.

This weakens the vein wall, resulting in a condition known as varicose veins. While the blood loss from a bleeding vein does not tend to be as quick as a bleeding artery, it does nonetheless have the potential to be a very serious and even fatal injury. Bleeding from a vein will seem to flow from an injury and because it has little or no oxygen it will appear to be a dark red.

Capillaries are very thin-walled vessels. Blood is forced through them under pressure, causing the nutrients and oxygen stored in the blood to be pushed out into the body tissues and organs.

TYPES OF INJURY Small blood loss is very common and rarely needs much treatment. Large blood loss may lead, if untreated, to shock and, potentially, death.

Incisions Clean and deep cuts characterized by paper cuts and knives are known as incisions. While these wounds do not tend to bleed a lot, there may be underlying damage to tendons and other tissues.

Lacerations are jagged wounds, which tend to bleed a lot.

Puncture wounds are, as their name suggests, deep injuries caused by a pointed object such as a knitting needle. They do not tend to bleed a great deal but they carry the risk of infection because dirt can be carried a long way into the tissue. There is also a greater risk of damage to vital organs such as the lungs or liver.

Scrapes are a commonplace injury and involve damage to the top layers of the skin. They do not cause major blood loss but are often dirty, because grazes tend to have debris embedded within them.

Puncture

Laceration

Graze

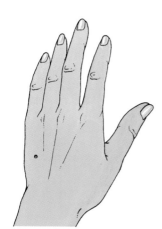

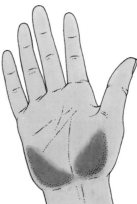

Above
Puncture wounds are holes caused by sharp objects such as nails or knitting needles. They do not bleed profusely but may carry dirt into body tissues, which may cause infection.

Above
Clean, deep cuts caused by knives or paper are known as incisions. The underlying tissues and tendons may be damaged, even though there may be little blood loss.

Above
A scrape occurs when the top layer of skin is damaged, usually caused by a fall. Scrapes rarely bleed much but often have debris embedded within them.

HOW DOES THE BODY STOP BLEEDING?

When a blood vessel is torn or cut, a series of chemical reactions takes place that causes the formation of a blood clot to seal the injury. Components of the blood known as platelets clump together at the injury site. Damaged tissue and platelets release chemicals that activate proteins called clotting factors. These react with a special protein (fibrinogen) to form a mesh of filaments that traps blood cells. These form the basis of a blood clot that contains white blood cells to help fight infection and specialized blood cells that help promote repair and recovery. A scab will form to protect the wound until repair has taken place. When applying pressure to the site of a wound you are helping the clotting process.

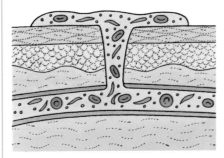

Above *When a blood vessel is damaged it constricts immediately to reduce blood flow and blood loss. Platelets stick to the blood vessel walls near the site of injury.*

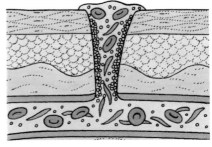

Above *Platelets clump together at the site of injury and, along with damaged tissue, release chemicals that begin a complex series of reactions involving clotting factors.*

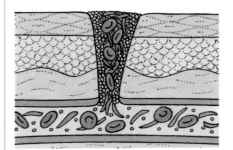

Above *The final part in the chemical process is the conversion of the protein fibrinogen, found in blood plasma, into sticky threads that trap cells.*

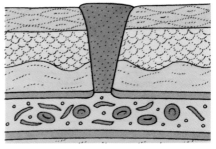

Above *Cells trapped in the mesh form a blood clot at the site of injury. Over time, the clot hardens to form a protective scab over the wound while healing takes place.*

Treatment of External Bleeding

Coming across somebody who is bleeding heavily can be very frightening. It may be reassuring to remember that many adults donate up to a pint of blood with no ill effects, and yet if this same amount were tipped onto the floor it would look very alarming. Serious shock in an adult tends to develop only after 2 pints of blood or more is lost from the body, and even this can be effectively treated with good first aid and early hospital care.

TREATMENT The three main principles of the treatment of external bleeding are:

- Look
- Apply direct pressure
- Elevate

1 Look at the wound to check how large it is. Check that the wound has nothing in it (such as debris or a foreign body).

2 Apply direct pressure to the wound. If the victim is able to press on the wound, encourage him or her to do so. If not, then apply direct pressure yourself, initially with your fingers and, if you have it handy, with a sterile dressing or a piece of clean cloth. Applying direct pressure to the wound enables the blood to clot and therefore stems the blood flow from the cut.

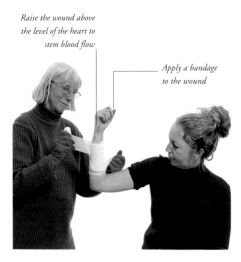

Raise the wound above the level of the heart to stem blood flow

Apply a bandage to the wound

Once applied, a sterile dressing (or whatever you have handy) should ideally be held in place with a firm bandage or improvised bandage such as a scarf or tie.

3 Elevate the wound. If the injury is on an arm or leg, raise the wound above the level of the heart. It is harder for the blood to pump upward and this therefore reduces the blood flow to the wound and thus the fluid loss from the body.

4 Treat for shock (see pages 44–45). Keep the victim warm and continually at rest. Reassure the victim.

PROTECTING YOURSELF

Whenever possible, you should avoid direct contact with blood or other body fluids such as vomit. This is to protect both you and the person that you are treating. There are several ways of doing this:

● If available, use gloves. These come in many different sizes and materials (particularly useful if you have an allergy to latex) and should be kept in every first aid kit.

● If the person bleeding is able, ask her to apply direct pressure to the injury herself.
● Use bandages, dressings, or other materials, such as a handkerchief or T-shirt, as a barrier between your hand and the wound.
● Keep injuries on your own hands covered with plasters or dressings.

If you do get blood on your skin, simply wash off well with soap and hot water. Clear up spills of blood or vomit with a bleach and water solution. Clothing that has been stained by blood or vomit should be put through a hot wash in the washing machine. If you are concerned about the possibility of infection after dealing with body fluids, contact your doctor. It is important to remember that the risk of cross-infection is minimal and that in most instances where you are applying first aid you will be doing so for a member of your own family.

Bleeding from the Head or Palm

Bleeding from the head is usually caused by a blow. The scalp in particular has a rich blood supply and even a small wound can bleed heavily. The palm of the hand is commonly cut while cutting objects or through a fall. Bleeding is often severe as the palm also has a rich blood supply. There are many tendons and nerves in the hand, and wounds to the palm may be accompanied by loss of movement or feeling in the fingers.

HOW TO TREAT HEAD BLEEDS

Treatment should include taking full details of what happened and checking for signs of head injury, such as skull fracture, concussion, or compression (see Fractures of the Skull, Face, and Jaw, pages 96–97).

1 Help the injured person to sit or lie down.

2 Check for any signs of head injury. Treat as appropriate.

3 Using a sterile bandage, apply direct pressure to the wound to stop the bleeding.

4 Cover the wound with a sterile dressing or a clean pad. Tie this in place with a bandage.

5 Take or send the victim to hospital as soon as possible.

If the victim becomes unconscious, monitor and maintain airway and breathing and be prepared to resuscitate as necessary (see pages 29–33).

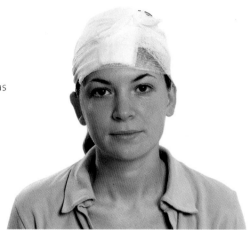

SIGNS AND SYMPTOMS OF SKULL FRACTURE, CONCUSSION, AND COMPRESSION

Skull fracture
- Bruising to the eye socket
- Pain
- A bump or dent in the skull
- Straw-colored fluid coming from one or both ears
- Victim becomes increasingly drowsy and unresponsive over a period of time. Does she respond slowly to questions or commands? Is she having problems focusing?

Concussion
- Pale skin
- Dizziness, blurred vision, or nausea
- Headache
- Brief or partial loss of consciousness

Compression
- Person becomes increasingly drowsy and unresponsive
- Flushed and dry skin
- Slurred speech and confusion
- Partial or total loss of movement, often down one side of the body
- One pupil appears to be larger than the other
- Noisy breathing, which becomes slow
- Slow, strong pulse

HOW TO TREAT BLEEDING FROM THE PALM

1 Help the victim to sit or lie down. Apply direct pressure to the wound and raise the arm. If the person has had a fall, take care to rule out a broken arm or collarbone before raising the arm.

2 Place a sterile dressing or clean pad in the hand and ask the victim to grip her fingers over it. Bandage the fingers so that they are clenched over the pad. Leave the thumb exposed. If there is an embedded object in the wound, treat the hand

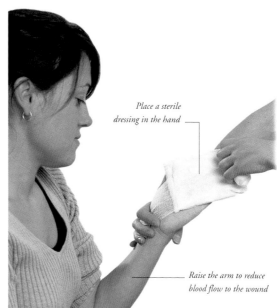

Place a sterile dressing in the hand

Raise the arm to reduce blood flow to the wound

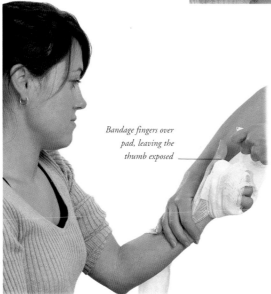

Bandage fingers over pad, leaving the thumb exposed

flat and bandage around the object. If tendon damage means that the fingers cannot be clenched, bandage the wound with the hand flat.

3 Treat for shock (see pages 44–45) if necessary. Keep the victim warm, at rest, and reassure him or her.

4 Support the arm in an elevation sling and take or send the victim to hospital.

Treating Chest or Abdominal Wounds

The chest wall protects the lungs, heart, and other essential organs such as the liver. A puncture wound to the chest can therefore be extremely serious. Wounds to the abdomen (stomach and intestines) are very serious. External bleeding may be severe and internal bleeding is likely, both of which will lead to serious shock. In addition, there may be damage to internal organs and the digestive system.

CHEST WOUNDS Common complications of penetrating chest wounds include:

● Collapsed lung (pneumothorax), caused by air entering the space between the chest wall and the lungs. This applies pressure to the lungs, causing them to collapse. The lung can also be damaged directly, causing it to fill with blood.
● Tension pneumothorax which occurs when the pressure builds up sufficiently to affect the uninjured lung and possibly even the heart.
● Damage to vital organs such as the liver—this will result in severe shock as these organs have a large blood supply.

TREATMENT

1 Seal the wound using, in the first instance, your hand or the victim's hand.

2 Help the victim into a position that makes it easier for him to breathe. This will usually be

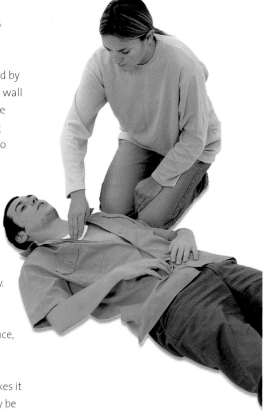

sitting up and inclined to the injured side. This allows the uninjured lung maximum room to move and allows blood to pool on the injured side.

3 Cover the wound with a dressing and cover the dressing with airtight material, such as plastic or foil. Seal this on three sides.

4 Call an ambulance and treat for shock (see pages 44–45).

If the victim is unconscious, monitor and maintain the airway, and be prepared to resuscitate (see pages 29–33) if necessary (sealing the wound before resuscitating). Place the victim injured side down.

SIGNS AND SYMPTOMS OF CHEST WOUNDS

- Difficulty with breathing
- Shock
- Bright red, frothy blood (blood with air in it) being coughed up or escaping from the wound
- Pale skin with blue lips
- Sound of air being sucked into the chest

TREATING ABDOMINAL WOUNDS

1 Call an ambulance and help the victim to lie down in the most comfortable position.

2 Consider the position of the wound. If it is vertical—runs down the abdomen—moving the victim so that he is lying flat on the ground will help bring the edges together, ease discomfort, and help reduce bleeding. If the wound is horizontal, gently raising the legs will have the same effect.

Below
A horizontal wound can be helped if you raise the victim's legs and support them with a rolled-up coat or blanket. This action will help close the edges of the wound and slow down the flow of blood.

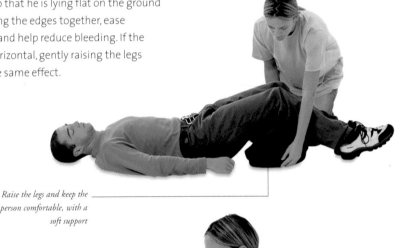

Raise the legs and keep the person comfortable, with a soft support

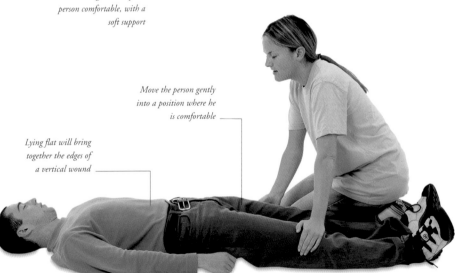

Move the person gently into a position where he is comfortable

Lying flat will bring together the edges of a vertical wound

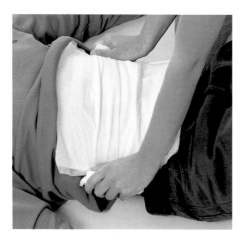

3 Place a large dressing over the wound and secure in place. Add pads to this dressing as necessary.

4 Treat for shock (see pages 44–45).

Support the wound if the victim coughs, vomits, or needs to be moved into the recovery position (see pages 20–23). Press lightly on the bandage to prevent intestines protruding from the wound. If intestines are protruding, do not attempt to replace them. Cover with a clean piece of plastic film.

MAJOR ORGANS

Damage to any of the body's major organs can be life-threatening and prompt action must therefore be taken to minimize the effects of injuries to the chest or abdomen. Even when external bleeding is slight, the risk of internal bleeding cannot be discounted. Knowing where in the body the organs are located will help a first responder to assess a situation and decide the most appropriate emergency treatment, and also to give accurate information when the emergency services arrive.

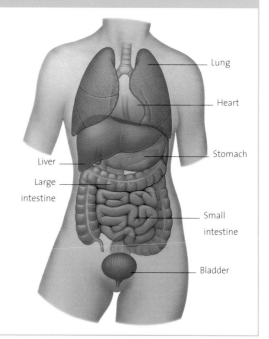

Lung

Heart

Stomach

Liver

Large intestine

Small intestine

Bladder

Crush Injuries, Impalement, and Amputation

Crush injuries generally result from serious car accidents or explosions. There may be part of the body trapped under heavy debris; several broken bones, multiple external bleeding and much internal bleeding; burns from an explosion; severe shock, and deterioration into unconsciousness. If a person is impaled on an immovable object, treatment is similar to that for a foreign object embedded in a wound (see pages 170–173). An amputation is where a part of the body has been severed. This may occur through a straight and heavy cut or through twisting and pulling under extreme force.

TREATING CRUSH INJURIES

1 Ensure that it is safe to approach the scene. If in doubt, call 911 and wait for help.

2 Monitor and maintain airway and breathing and be prepared to resuscitate if necessary (see pages 29–33).

3 Treat major bleeding and cover smaller wounds with sterile dressings.

4 Keep the injured person still and try to reassure him or her while waiting for help.

5 Treat for shock (see pages 44–45).

6 Make an early call for an ambulance and inform medical staff what has happened.

IF THE INJURED PERSON IS TRAPPED There are additional risks for the injured person if any part of the body is trapped. Releasing the body may bring on severe shock as fluid leaks to the injured part.

An even greater cause for concern is "crush syndrome." Toxins build up around the injury site and are trapped by an object crushing the person. If the object is removed, these toxins are suddenly released into the body, and the kidneys, the organs chiefly responsible for flushing out toxins, are overwhelmed. This condition can be fatal.

IF THE PERSON HAS BEEN TRAPPED FOR LESS THAN 10 MINUTES Crush syndrome takes some time to develop. If you can do so, safely remove the object. Treat as for crush injuries (above.)

IF THE PERSON HAS BEEN TRAPPED FOR LONGER THAN 10 MINUTES Make an early call for help, explaining the situation, but do not remove the object. Treat as for crush injuries (left) and reassure the person.

Monitor and maintain airway and breathing

Remove object if possible

TREATING IMPALEMENT

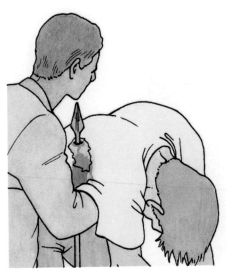

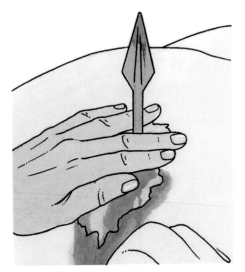

1 Do not attempt to remove the object or to move the injured person.

2 Provide swift assistance for the injured person, supporting his body weight where possible to prevent any further damage.

3 If bleeding is severe, apply pressure around the edges of the wound without pressing on the object.

4 Try to stop the object moving around as much as possible, enlisting bystander support where available.

5 Call an ambulance, making sure that you explain the need for cutting equipment or tools.

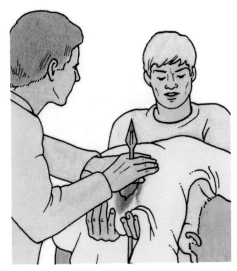

6 Treat for shock (see pages 44–45) as best you can.

TREATING AMPUTATION

 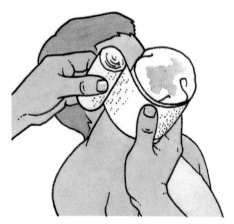

1 Your priority is to stop any bleeding at the site of the injury. Apply direct pressure and raise the injured stump. An amputation high on the arm or leg can be accompanied by severe arterial bleeding, particularly if caused by a twisting or tearing movement. Be prepared to apply continuous pressure using several pads as necessary.

2 If the bleeding comes under control, cover the wound with a sterile dressing or clean non-fluffy material tied in place with a bandage.

3 Treat for shock (see pages 44–45) and reassure the person.

4 Call 911, advising that there is an amputation.

FOR THE AMPUTATED PART
A surgeon may be able to reattach the amputated part.

1 Wrap the part in a plastic bag and wrap the bag in a clean cloth.

2 Place the cloth-wrapped bag in ice and place into a sturdy container. Do not let the ice come into close contact with the amputated part, because this will damage the flesh. Do not wash the amputated part.

3 Label the container with the time of injury and the victim's name and make sure that you personally hand it over to medical staff.

Internal Bleeding

Severe internal bleeding is a potentially life-threatening condition. While the blood may not be obvious, it is still lost from the circulatory system and the victim is therefore very likely to go into shock (see pages 44–45). Internal bleeding may also cause a build-up of pressure that, in areas such as the skull or around the heart, can cause serious problems, loss of consciousness and, if untreated, lead to death.

SITES OF BLEEDING Internal bleeding can be very difficult to identify. It is not unusual for internal bleeding to happen slowly, with signs and symptoms showing up days after an accident. It can happen to any part of the body but the richness of the blood supply in the stomach, around the organs such as the liver and the spleen, and in the bowel make these sites particularly vulnerable.

Internal bleeding is also likely to accompany some broken bones. The thigh bone protects the femoral artery and if broken may pierce it, causing a large and life-threatening bleed.

TREATMENT

1 Treat for shock (see pages 44–45). Keep the person warm. Place him in a comfortable position, preferably lying down with the legs slightly raised. Reassure him. Treat any external bleeding or bleeding from orifices.

2 Call 911 as soon as possible and explain what has happened.

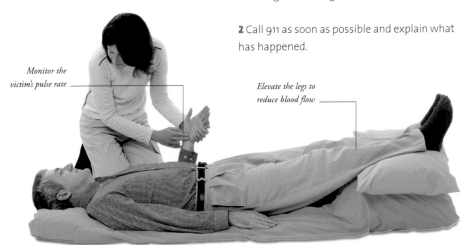

Monitor the victim's pulse rate

Elevate the legs to reduce blood flow

MAJOR ORGANS SUSCEPTIBLE TO INTERNAL BLEEDING

Internal bleeding can happen in any part of the body but the stomach, the liver, spleen, and intestines are particularly vulnerable because they have a rich blood supply. Internal bleeding can be very difficult to identify and signs and symptoms may not arise until several days after an accident has occurred.

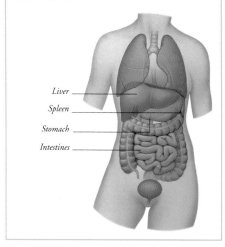

Liver

Spleen

Stomach

Intestines

Monitor and record the person's pulse and breathing rates. This information will be useful for the medical staff in determining the extent of the injury.

If the person becomes unconscious, place in the recovery position (see pages 22–25) and monitor airway and breathing. Be prepared to resuscitate if necessary (see pages 30–33).

SIGNS AND SYMPTOMS

● The person is known to have had an accident (not necessarily in the immediate past)
● Signs and symptoms of shock (see pages 44–45)
● Bruising
● Boarding—this most commonly occurs where there is bleeding into the stomach area; the quantity of blood combined with the tissues swelling result in a rigidity to the tissues
● Swelling
● Bleeding from body orifices (see Bleeding from Special Sites, pages 87–89)

If there is any combination of these signs and symptoms, suspect internal bleeding.

BRUISING

Less serious internal bleeding such as small bruises can be treated with a cold compress to relieve pain and reduce swelling. However, the possibility of further internal bleeding or underlying injury should not be ruled out, particularly if the victim is known, for example, to have hit his head on a window during a traffic accident, or has been hit in the stomach by a reversing automobile. For more information on bruising, see Minor Wounds, pages 161–164.

Eye Wounds and Embedded Objects

Cuts to the eye can be very frightening and even small, difficult to notice injuries are potentially very serious. However, medical treatments mean that even injuries that appear to be very severe may not necessarily result in the loss of sight in the eye. Do not touch the affected eye.

TREATMENT

Prevent further injury and get medical help as soon as possible.

1 Lie the person down, on his back if possible, and hold the head to prevent movement and keep it stable.

2 Ask the person to try to keep his eyes still to prevent movement of the injured eye. Ask the person to focus on something to prevent movement.

3 Ask the victim to hold a clean pad over the eye to help prevent movement and infection. If the wait for an ambulance

Hold the head to prevent movement

SIGNS AND SYMPTOMS OF EYE WOUNDS
● Knowing that something has impacted with the eye—this could be as small as a grain of sand or a splinter
● Pain in the eye
● Loss or limitation of vision
● Bleeding

or other help may take some time, you may wish to hold the pad for the person or to gently bandage it in place. However, because blood loss from the eye area is not likely to be life-threatening, any bandage should be used only to hold the pad in place and not to apply pressure.

Do not attempt to remove any object embedded in the eye. If the object is very long, then gently support it to prevent movement at its base. If small, ensure that the pad you place over the eye does not push it in any further.

TREATING AN OBJECT EMBEDDED IN THE WOUND

The first step in the treatment of any external bleeding is to check the extent of the injury and see if there is anything embedded in the wound.

1 Apply pressure around the edges of the wound using your hands or the victim's hands without pressing on the object.

2 Replace this pressure with a dressing or clean material and bandage firmly in place, avoiding pressure on the object.

3 Raise the injured limb if possible to staunch the flow of blood.

4 Prevent longer objects from moving by supporting them with your hands or by packing around the base of the object with blankets, for example.

WARNING

If there is something stuck into the injury, do not attempt to remove it because:

● If the object went in at an angle, you may cause more damage pulling it out
● You may leave splinters in the wound
● The object may be pressing against a vein or an artery, reducing blood loss
● You may have mistaken a broken bone for a foreign body

The principles of applying pressure, elevating, and treating for shock (see pages 44–45) still apply.

Place a sterile dressing over the wound

5 Treat for shock (see pages 44–45) and reassure the victim.

If the victim is impaled on something which cannot be moved, support him or her to stop from pulling on the impaled object and causing further damage. Where possible, treat the victim as described on pages 84–85, and ensure that the emergency team is aware of the need for cutting equipment. For further information on impalement, see page 80.

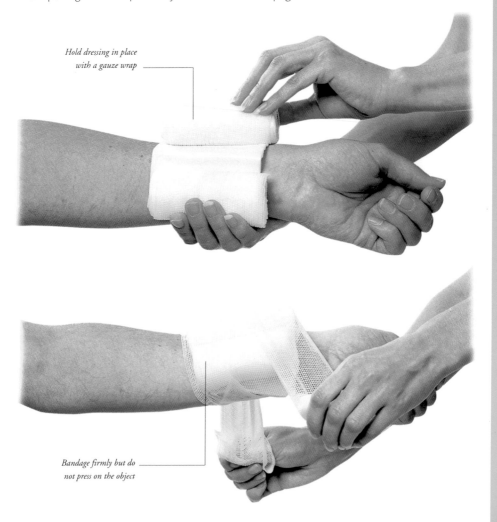

Hold dressing in place with a gauze wrap

Bandage firmly but do not press on the object

Bleeding from Special Sites

Bleeding from bodily orifices includes nosebleeds, bleeding from the ear, mouth, vagina, anus, and urethra. It may be an indication of a serious disorder.

NOSEBLEED Nosebleeds are very common and often the cause is unknown. For general treatment of uncomplicated nosebleed, see How to Treat Nosebleeds, page 89, and Controlling Bleeding from the Mouth and Nose, pages 90–91. If a bleeding follows a heavy impact to the nose, then assume that there may be a broken nose or cheekbone (see Fractures of the Skull, Face, and Jaw, pages 96–97).

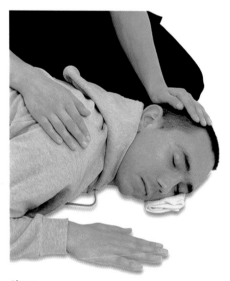

Above

If there is blood loss from the ear, keep the victim as still as possible and rest the head with the injured side down, with a clean pad held over the ear into which the blood can drain.

BLEEDING FROM THE EAR If the blood from the ear is thin and watery then it is likely that there has been some damage to the skull, and possibly the brain, since the blood is mixing with the fluid that cushions the brain. This is a very serious injury and 911 should be called as soon as possible. Keep the victim as still as you can and gently rest the head, injured ear down, with a clean pad held over the ear for the blood to drain into. Do not tie this pad in place. Keep a check on the victim's airway and breathing (see pages 12–13) and be prepared to resuscitate if necessary (see pages 29–33).

If the blood is bright red and is accompanied by earache, deafness, a sudden change in pressure, or an explosion then it is likely to be a burst eardrum. Again, keep the injured ear downward, hold a clean pad in place, and seek medical attention.

BLEEDING FROM THE MOUTH If bleeding from the mouth follows a direct impact to the face it is likely that the bleeding has been caused by damage to the teeth, gums, or tongue. There may also be damage to the jaw and cheekbones (see Controlling Bleeding from the Mouth and Nose, pages 90–91). Bright red and frothy bleeding from the mouth may be a sign of damage to the lungs (see Chest and Abdominal Wounds, pages 74–75).

Dark red blood being coughed up from the mouth may be a sign of a burst stomach ulcer. Seek urgent medical attention.

BLEEDING FROM THE VAGINA The most likely reason for vaginal bleeding is menstruation (a period). If this is the case and the bleed is accompanied by cramps then a woman may wish to take her normal analgesics.

A woman complaining of vaginal bleeding not related to her periods should be given privacy and sensitive handling, with gentle questioning to determine the cause. For all vaginal bleeding, provide sanitary pads or a clean towel where possible. Where the bleeding is potentially pregnancy-related, do not dispose of old pads of any blood loss.

Instead, move these discreetly away from the woman to be checked by medical staff.

Bleeding in early pregnancy may be an indication of a miscarriage, but there are a number of other potential causes. Make the woman comfortable and seek advice from her midwife or doctor. If the bleeding is severe and/or she is displaying signs of shock (see pages 44–45), call 911.

In later pregnancy a bright red, painless bleed may indicate a serious problem with the placenta. Make the woman comfortable, call 911 and treat for shock.

If the bleeding is as a result of an accident or recent assault, call 911 and treat for shock.

Right

A woman with vaginal bleeding needs to be treated sensitively. Provide clean towels or sanitary pads, and keep these for medical staff to check if you suspect a miscarriage.

HOW TO TREAT NOSEBLEEDS IN ADULTS

1 Lean forward and spit blood into a handkerchief or some other receptacle.

2 Pinch the nose just below the bone and apply firm pressure for 10 minutes (this is the amount of time it takes for a clot to form). If the bleeding has not stopped after 10 minutes, apply pressure for two further periods of 10 minutes. If it is still bleeding then either take or send the victim to hospital.

Once the bleeding has stopped, advise the victim not to scratch, pick, or blow his nose, not to drink hot liquid, and not to exert himself, as all these activities can dislodge the clot and cause the bleeding to start again.

BLEEDING FROM THE ANUS Bleeding from the anus may be bright red and fresh looking. If it follows a recent accident, this may indicate injury to the anus or lower bowel. Treat for shock as appropriate and seek medical help.

Black, tarry blood has been partially digested and indicates a potential injury to the upper bowel. Again, treat for shock as appropriate and seek medical help.

BLEEDING FROM THE URETHRA Blood in the urine, particularly following an accident, may indicate injury to the bladder, kidneys, or other internal organs. It may also accompany a broken pelvis where the bone has damaged the bladder. Treat for shock as appropriate and seek medical help as quickly as possible. There is no way of determining the seriousness of the situation until it is in expert hands.

Controlling Bleeding from the Mouth and Nose

There are a number of potential reasons for bleeding from the mouth. If bleeding is a result of direct impact to the face, there are likely to be injuries to the jaw and possibly the cheekbone, as well as to the gums and teeth. It may also be that bleeding follows dental treatment. In the case of nosebleeds, find out what caused the nosebleed so you can establish whether the nose or cheekbone has been damaged. Many nosebleeds start spontaneously and the cause is never known. The priority with any mouth or nosebleed is to protect the victim's airway and try to prevent blood being swallowed because this may cause vomiting.

HOW TO TREAT BLEEDING FROM THE MOUTH

1 Lean the victim forward and encourage her to spit out any blood and/or broken teeth into a receptacle.

2 If the bleed is easy to reach, controlling it may be helped by placing a small dressing over the wound and encouraging the victim to apply pressure for 10 minutes.

3 If there is severe bleeding from a tooth socket, place a rolled-up dressing, large enough to stop the teeth from meeting, into the mouth

Spit out blood and teeth into a bowl

and ask the person to bite on it. If this does not control the bleeding after 10 minutes, reapply a clean pad.

If the bleeding has not stopped after 30 minutes, or is particularly severe, either take or send the victim to hospital. There may be damage to the jaw or cheekbone. Cold compresses may relieve this pain and reduce swelling and you may need to support broken bones with pads or your hands (see also Fractures of the Skull, Face, and Jaw, pages 96–97).

IF THE NOSE OR CHEEK APPEARS TO BE BROKEN

Lean the victim forward and encourage him to spit out blood. Do not pinch the nose. Cold compresses either side of the injury may provide some relief and help to reduce the bleeding.

IF A TOOTH HAS BEEN KNOCKED OUT

Adult teeth can sometimes be replanted in the mouth, so it is worth storing the tooth carefully. Do not wash the tooth; instead, place it in a labeled plastic bag with some milk or water to keep it moist, and send with the person to the emergency dentist or hospital. Teeth need to be replanted quickly—go to a dentist or hospital emergency room.

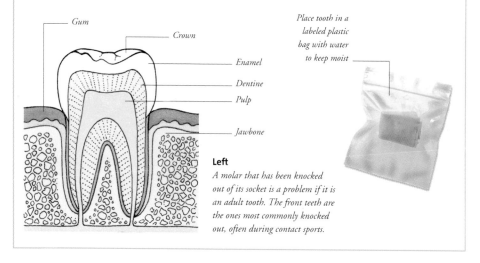

Gum

Crown

Enamel

Dentine

Pulp

Jawbone

Place tooth in a labeled plastic bag with water to keep moist

Left
A molar that has been knocked out of its socket is a problem if it is an adult tooth. The front teeth are the ones most commonly knocked out, often during contact sports.

Fractures, Dislocations, and Soft Tissue Injuries

Fracture is just another word for a broken bone. A dislocation occurs at the site of a joint and is where a bone is fully or partially displaced. Soft tissue injuries include sprains, strains, and ruptures. They are often caused in the same way as fractures and generally are hard to distinguish from broken bones.

BROKEN BONES There are two main types of broken bone. The first is a closed (simple) break or fracture, where the bone has broken but has not pierced the skin. A closed fracture is sometimes difficult to diagnose, even for experienced medical staff, who will usually rely on an X-ray to determine whether or not the bone is definitely broken. The second type is an open (compound) break or fracture, where the bone has either pierced the skin or is associated with an open wound. The greatest risk with open breaks is infection. Both open and closed breaks can result in injury to underlying organs or blood vessels and may also be unstable if the ends of the broken bone are moving around. In young children the bones are not fully formed and may bend rather than break (termed a greenstick fracture).

While it is possible to give some general guidance for the recognition of broken bones, no two people are identical in their response. The first general rule therefore is, if in doubt, assume that a bone is broken and treat as such.

Be particularly aware of potential fractures if the accident involved a sharp blow, a fall, a rapid increase or decrease of speed, or a sudden twist.

DISLOCATIONS The most common sites for dislocations are the shoulders, thumbs, and hips. Dislocations are usually characterized by intense pain and an obvious deformity. There may be signs and symptoms similar to a broken bone, including feelings of tingling or numbness below the site of the injury, caused by trapped nerves or blood vessels. Do not attempt to replace the bone. Make the victim comfortable and take or send him to hospital.

SOFT TISSUE INJURIES Strains are an overstretching of the muscle, leading to a partial tear. Ruptures are complete tears in muscles. Sprains are injuries to a ligament at or near a joint. The signs and symptoms of soft tissue injuries will be similar to the signs and symptoms of a fracture and will generally follow a sharp twisting or stretching movement.

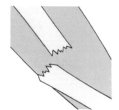

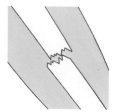

Above

If a long bone in the arm or leg bends it may crack on one side only, known as a greenstick fracture. This type of fracture only occurs in children, whose bones are still flexible.

Above

When the broken bone pierces the skin it is known as an open or compound fracture. There is a risk of infection and increased damage to nerves and blood vessels.

Above

In a closed or simple fracture the bone does not break through the skin. If the break is straight across the bone (usually in the arm or leg) it is known as a transverse fracture.

Above

Sometimes a bone may crack rather than break, usually as a result of repeated jarring of a bone such as may occur in the shinbones of long-distance runners.

SIGNS AND SYMPTOMS OF BROKEN BONES

Pain This accompanies most, but not all, fractures and is caused by the broken bone ends pressing on nerve endings.

Deformity An injured part may appear deformed, particularly when compared to the uninjured side.

Swelling Some swelling may be present at the site of a fracture.

Tenderness This accompanies most broken bones and can often only be felt when the injured part is gently touched.

Shock The signs and symptoms of shock (see pages 44–45) will often accompany major fractures. There may be reddening or bruising over the site of the break, but this often takes some time to appear. You may also hear the ends of broken bone rubbing together, a sound known as crepitus.

Another potential sign of a broken bone is a lack of feeling or a tingling sensation below the fracture site. This may indicate nerve damage or a reduction in circulation caused by the bone pushing on either the nerves or the blood vessels. The treatment for injuries displaying these symptoms is the same as for any broken bone. However, if you have been trained to do so, applying traction may alleviate the problem.

If the victim is displaying any combination of these signs and symptoms or the nature of the accident suggests that a fracture is likely, assume that a bone is broken.

How to Treat Fractures

The general rule for treating all broken bones is to immobilize them, because this reduces pain and the likelihood of further injury. The risk of infection is also an important consideration in the treatment of open fractures and requires action. Do not give a person who has a broken bone anything to eat or drink in case he needs a general anesthetic in hospital.

KEEPING A BROKEN BONE STILL

1 The victim will often have put the injured part in the position that is most comfortable for him and will generally be guarding the injury and keeping it still. If the victim has not done this, encourage him to keep still and help him into a comfortable position.

2 Once the victim is still you can help to steady and support the fracture using your hands. By helping the victim keep the injured part still you enable him to relax. The very act of relaxing the muscles reduces the pull on the broken bones and often alleviates pain.

3 If you have to transport the victim yourself, or if it is going to be a while until help arrives, then you can immobilize the broken bone further with bandages or improvise with coats or blankets, for example.

The key points to remember with any type of bandaging are:

● Not to tie the bandage too tightly.
● To pad around the site of the break.

Do not move the injured area unnecessarily.

Bandage the break if the victim is to be transported

1 Place the dressing over the wound and build up padding alongside the bone.

2 Tie both the padding and the dressing in place, using firm pressure.

3 Remember that broken bones do swell and that you may need to loosen the bandage if the circulation below the site of the break becomes impaired.

TREATMENT OF OPEN BREAKS In the first instance, the wound should be protected using either a sterile dressing or an improvised dressing made from a piece of clean, dry, and non-fluffy material. If the bleeding is profuse, or you are going to have to wait some time for further help, this dressing should be held in place using the same principles as you would apply if there were a foreign object in the wound (see page 85).

CHECKING FOR DAMAGE TO CIRCULATION

With any bandaging, you run the risk of cutting off the circulation to the area below the site of the bandage. While this can in part be avoided by not tying bandages too tightly and by never using a tourniquet, the nature of wounds means that they swell and this can cause a once satisfactory bandage to become too tight. There are a number of ways to check whether a bandage is cutting off the circulation:

● If the skin below the site of the bandage becomes white, gray, or blue, or feels cold to the touch.
● If the victim complains of tingling, numbness, or of a lack of circulation.
● If the pulse in the limb slows or stops.
● If the color does not quickly return to the skin after the skin is gently pinched or the nail compressed.

If you notice any of these signs, gently loosen, but do not remove, the bandage until the blood flow returns.

Fractures of the Skull, Face, and Jaw

A skull fracture is a very serious injury since it is often associated with some form of damage to the brain. Concussion and compression may both accompany skull fractures. If a person has a fracture to the bones of the face or jaw, the airway is your overwhelming priority.

TREATING A FRACTURED SKULL

1 Keep the victim still while she is conscious. Encourage her not to move her head.

2 Keep a constant check on the airway, breathing, and circulation (see pages 12–17).

3 Be prepared to resuscitate (see page 29–33) or turn into the recovery position (see pages 20–23) if necessary.

4 Call for emergency help as soon as possible.

HOW TO TREAT FRACTURES OF THE FACE AND JAW

1 Ensure that any blood in the mouth is allowed to dribble out—encourage the victim to spit into a bandage or handkerchief.

2 Gently remove any teeth or bits of broken bone from the mouth and give the victim a pad to hold against the injured part for additional support and comfort.

3 A cold compress may help to reduce pain.

4 Get the victim to hospital because she will require medical treatment.

5 Do not pinch a broken nose to control bleeding—hold a pad under it.

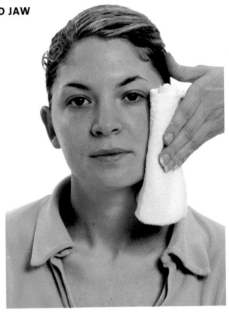

SIGNS AND SYMPTOMS OF A SKULL FRACTURE

Along with these signs and symptoms, consider what happened. Skull fractures may be caused by direct and heavy impact to the head or by indirect impact, for example, a fall from a great height on to the feet that may have caused the force to move up the body, stopping when it hit the skull.

● Bruising to the eye socket
● Pain
● A bump or a dent

● Straw-colored fluid coming from one or both ears
● Deterioration in the level of consciousness of the victim

Does the person respond slowly to questions or commands? Is he having problems focusing?

If any of these things is present, assume a skull fracture with a potential injury to the brain.

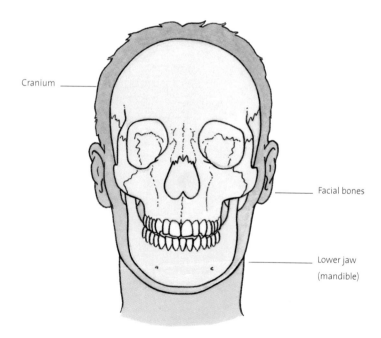

Cranium

Facial bones

Lower jaw
(mandible)

Concussion

In itself, concussion is not a serious injury as the victim will recover when the disturbance caused by the impact stops. However, because concussion often accompanies violent head movement, there is always the possibility of a skull fracture or more serious, longer-term brain injury, such as compression. It is important therefore that even a seemingly recovered victim with concussion should seek medical treatment.

HOW TO TREAT CONCUSSION

1 Place the victim in the recovery position if necessary and monitor ABC.

2 Call an ambulance if the victim does not recover after 3 minutes or if there are signs of skull fracture or compression.

3 Advise the victim to seek medical advice if recovery appears to be complete.

4 Encourage the victim to keep still while recovering because this reduces dizziness and nausea.

5 Be aware of the increased likelihood of neck injuries.

COMPRESSION

Compression is a very serious injury that occurs when pressure is exerted on the

brain, either by a piece of bone, bleeding, or swelling of the injured brain. It may develop immediately after a head injury or stroke, or some hours or even days later.

SIGNS AND SYMPTOMS OF COMPRESSION

- Person becomes increasingly drowsy and unresponsive.
- Flushed and dry skin.
- Slurred speech and confusion.
- Partial or total loss of movement, often down one side of the body.
- One pupil bigger than the other.
- Noisy breathing which becomes slow.
- Slow, strong pulse.

HOW TO TREAT COMPRESSION

If some or all of these symptoms are present, suspect compression and carry out the following treatment.

1 If the victim is unconscious, place in the recovery position and monitor airway, breathing, and circulation (see pages 12–17).

2 If conscious, lay the victim down with the head and shoulders slightly raised, maintaining a close check on the ABC. Call an ambulance, and be prepared to resuscitate (see pages 24–28).

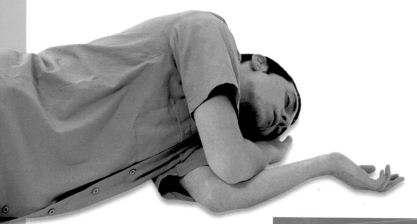

WARNING

Do not give anything to eat or drink—the victim may need a general anesthetic in hospital.

Fractures of the Upper Body

The collarbone can be broken by direct impact. However, it is most commonly fractured by indirect force moving up the arm following a fall on to an outstretched hand, and often happens after a fall from a bicycle or a horse. A broken shoulder often follows a heavy impact to the site of injury. It is therefore important to do a careful examination to rule out back or rib injury.

BROKEN COLLARBONE Along with potential swelling, bruising, and tenderness above the site of the injury, the victim is most likely to be supporting the injured arm, with the shoulder on the injured side slumped. Since the collarbone is close to the skin it is particularly important to look for an open fracture.

BROKEN SHOULDER If you are confident that the shoulder itself is broken then the treatment is to work with the victim to find the best position. The application of an arm sling (see Fractures of the Arm and Hand, pages 103–105) may provide some support, but more commonly the victim will want no bandages, settling instead for steady support from another person if available. The pain of the injury may make it necessary to call for an ambulance rather than transporting the victim to hospital in a car.

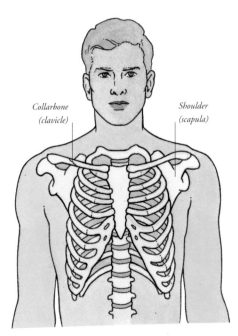

Collarbone
(clavicle)

Shoulder
(scapula)

WARNING
Do not give anything to eat or drink— the victim may need a general anesthetic in hospital.

Left
A broken collarbone often happens following a fall from a bicycle or a horse rather than direct impact. Use an elevation sling to take the weight of the arm and relieve pressure on the collarbone. It is important to check for an open fracture as the collarbone is close to the skin and may easily puncture it.

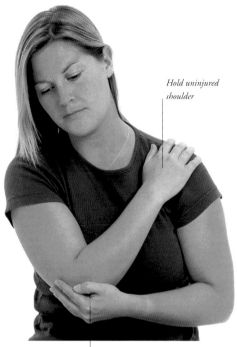

Hold uninjured
shoulder

Support elbow to reduce
pressure on collarbone

TREATMENT If the bone has pierced the skin, place a light dressing over the wound. Bleeding is likely to be minimal and your main concern is to prevent infection.

Work with the injured person to find the most comfortable position for the arm and for the body as a whole. Generally this will be sitting up with the arm supported at the elbow. The victim may wish to go to hospital in this position, but she should be offered the option of an elevation sling, which will help alleviate pressure on the collarbone and provide some comfort.

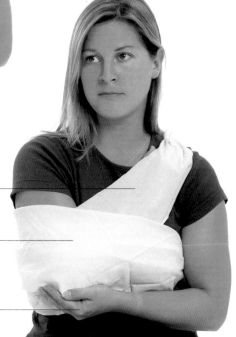

Place a bandage around
the body for extra support

Use a triangular bandage
to make an elevation sling

Keep the arm
supported at the elbow

APPLYING AN ELEVATION SLING The elevation sling has a range of uses. As well as the treatment of a broken collarbone, it also provides comfort in the treatment of crushed or broken fingers and hands, relief in the treatment of burns to the arm, and is an aid in controlling bleeding through elevation.

1 Place the injured arm with the fingers by the collarbone on the uninjured side.

2 Place the triangular bandage with the point resting at the elbow on the injured side.

3 Tuck the bandage underneath the hand and down underneath the injured arm.

4 Tie at the collarbone in a square knot (or a bow).

5 Fasten the spare material at the elbow with a pin or twist it and tuck it away.

6 Extra support can be gained by placing a triangular bandage folded into three (a broad fold) around the arm and body.

Fractures of the Arm and Hand

There are three long bones in each arm—one in the upper arm and two below the elbow. These are among the most commonly broken bones in the body. There is also a number of small bones in the wrist that are vulnerable to breaks. Fractures to the hand or fingers can be extremely painful because of the many nerve endings.

The principles of treatment are, as for all broken bones, to provide support to the injured part and to stop it from moving too much. Most people with a broken arm will be able to make their own way to the hospital or a health center, so treatment focuses on providing support that is appropriate when walking and stabilizes the injured limb. This can be done with an improvised sling using clothing, or by using a triangular bandage to form an arm sling.

Top end of bandage is put around the neck

HOW TO MAKE AN ARM SLING

1 Gently place the bandage under the victim's arm, placing the point underneath the elbow.

2 Pass the top end of the bandage around the back of the victim's neck, leaving a short end to be tied by the collarbone on the injured side.

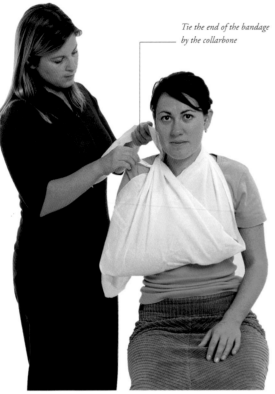

Tie the end of the bandage by the collarbone

3 Bring the bottom end of the bandage up carefully, ensuring that it fully supports the injured arm. Tie into place with a square knot or bow.

4 For additional support, you can tie another triangular bandage. Fold into three (a broad fold) around the arm, avoiding the site of the fracture, to stop the arm from moving.

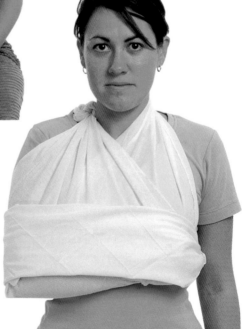

BROKEN ELBOW OR AN ARM THAT CANNOT BEND If the broken bone is on or near the elbow it may not be possible for the person to bend the arm, either because of the pain or because the joint is fixed. In this case you need to treat the arm in the position found—do not try to bend the arm.

1 Help the victim into the most comfortable position; this will often be lying down on the ground, but it may also be standing up with the arm hanging straight down.

2 Place padding around the injured part, both between the arm and the body and on the outside of the arm.

3 The victim will need to be transported by ambulance. Do not attempt to bandage the arm if help is on its way because this will cause further discomfort and may make the injury worse.

FRACTURED WRIST In older adults, the wrist may be broken by a fall onto an outstretched hand, causing a break very low down on the radius (one of the long bones in the lower arm) known as a Colles's or silver fork fracture. Other injuries can break one of the small bones to the wrist or cause a sprain that is particularly difficult to distinguish from a break.

TREATMENT Provide support and immobilization in the same way as for a break to the upper or lower arm. Remove watches and bracelets because these may contribute to cutting off circulation to the hand if the injury swells.

HAND FRACTURES Direct impact may break one or two of the small bones in the palm or fingers. Crushing injuries may break several bones and cause considerable bleeding. In addition the thumb, and even some of the fingers, may become dislocated.

TREATMENT

1 Gently cover any open wounds with a dressing or clean, non-fluffy piece of material. Encourage the victim to raise her arm. This helps to reduce swelling and bleeding and also provides some pain relief.

2 If possible, remove rings and wrist-watches before the injury starts to swell. If jewellery has been crushed into the hand or swelling prevents its easy removal, pass this information on as soon as possible to the medical staff as early treatment will be needed to prevent damage to the circulation in the fingers.

3 Cover the injured area with a pad of soft fabric or cotton wool (taking particular care if there are open wounds not to get strands of material stuck into the injury). This padding can be held in place with a cover created from a triangular bandage, which can also be adapted for crush injuries to the foot and for burns to the hand or foot.

Fractures of the Ribcage

Simple fractures, characterized by bruising and tenderness over the fracture site, are usually confined to one broken rib, with no underlying damage to the lungs or to other internal organs. Multiple, or complicated, rib fractures will often result in the victim having difficulty in breathing, as the chest wall is unable to move effectively. There may also be lung damage. Broken ribs are generally not strapped up because the chest needs to expand normally during breathing to reduce the risk of pneumonia.

TREATING A SIMPLE BROKEN RIB The best treatment for a simple fractured rib is to put the arm on the injured side into an arm sling and to advise the victim to seek medical aid.

MULTIPLE BROKEN RIBS In a case of multiple rib fractures there may also be lung damage, in which one or a number of ribs have punctured one or both of the lungs. There may also be an open break on the chest wall where ribs have sprung out. Remember that the ribs extend around the back of the body and there may be injuries here as well as on the front. Rib injuries may be accompanied by a sucking wound to the chest, creating a direct passage between the external environment and the lungs.

1 Treat any sucking wounds by covering, initially with a hand and then with plastic (see also Treating Chest or Abdominal Wounds, pages 74–77). Treat any open breaks.

2 If the victim is conscious, lay him down. He is most likely to find breathing easier in a half-sitting position.

Cover wound and help victim sit comfortably

SIGNS AND SYMPTOMS
OF MULTIPLE BROKEN RIBS

- Chest rises on the injured side as the person breathes out (paradoxical breathing)
- Swelling or indentation along the line of the ribs
- Open breaks
- Difficulty in breathing
- Pain on breathing
- Shock (as there is likely to be some degree of internal bleeding)
- Bright red, frothy blood coming from the mouth and/or nose. (This is an indication of a punctured lung as oxygenated blood is escaping from the respiratory system. There may or may not be an associated sucking wound to the chest)
- Sucking wound to the chest

3 Lean the victim toward the injured side. This allows any blood to drain into the injured lung, leaving the good lung free to breathe. Place the arm on the injured side into an elevation sling.

4 Treat for shock (see pages 44–45).

If the victim loses consciousness, monitor the airway and breathing (see pages 12–17) and place the person into the recovery position (see pages 20–23) with the injured side upward.

WARNING

Do not give anything to eat or drink—the victim may need a general anesthetic in hospital.

An elevation sling should be applied to the injured side

Recognizing Back and Spinal Injury

The spine is made up of a number of small bones called vertebrae. These form the backbone or spinal column, through which runs the spinal cord (the part of the central nervous system connecting all parts of the body with the brain) and major blood vessels. Injuries to the back are caused in a number of ways: through direct impact (such as a heavy blow to the neck or back); indirect impact (landing on the head or feet without bending the legs, thus allowing the force to travel up the body); and whiplash, when the head is violently thrown forward and backward (common in traffic accidents).

COMPLICATIONS WITH BACK INJURY The biggest danger with back injuries is the risk of nerve damage. The spinal cord containing the spinal nerves runs down the center of the vertebrae and fractures can sever or pinch these nerves, leading to partial or full paralysis. If the fracture is high in the neck, breathing may stop. Displaced vertebrae or swelling due to blood loss can also apply pressure to the spinal cord, leading to nerve damage.

Not all broken backs result in immediate damage to the spinal cord. However, the risk of spinal cord injuries is greatly increased if bones are broken, and any suspected fracture of the spine should be treated with extreme care.

Suspect a broken back or potential nerve damage if the accident involved:

- Rapid slowing down of movement.
- A fall from a height.
- A sharp blow directly to the back.
- Injury to the face or skull (because this often results from the head being thrown backward and forward).

SIGNS AND SYMPTOMS OF A BROKEN BACK

- Dent or step in the spine, which may indicate a displaced vertebra
- Bruising or swelling over the backbone
- Complaint of pain in the back
- Tenderness over the area of the break

TREATMENT Any spinal injury is potentially serious and you should seek emergency assistance immediately. The treatment for injuries to the back is to keep the injured person still while monitoring and maintaining airway and breathing (see pages 12–17). The general rule for dealing with broken bones or spinal cord damage is to keep the victim in the position that you found him until a doctor arrives, taking particular care to ensure the head is immobilized.

Unless the person is in danger or unconscious and requires resuscitation, do not move him from the position in which he was found. If you have been trained to do so, you can move the head into the neutral position before immobilization. Remain in this position until emergency help arrives.

1 If the victim is conscious and already lying down, leave him where he is. If the victim is still walking around, support him in lying down on the ground. If you can, put a blanket or coat underneath before you lie the person down.

2 Ensure that an ambulance has been called at the earliest opportunity.

3 Tell the person to keep still until medical help arrives and reassure him.

4 Hold the victim's head still by placing your hands over the ears and your fingers along the jawline.

5 Do not remove your support from the head until help arrives.

If the victim is unconscious, maintaining a clear airway is your first priority. See Unconscious Victim, page 116.

*Victim's nose
should be in line
with the navel*

Left
If spinal injury is suspected, the safest position for a person to be in is with the head, neck, and spine aligned. To check alignment, make sure that the victim's nose is in line with his navel. Keep the head immobilized.

BACK PAIN There are many causes of back pain. Among the most serious is damage to the spinal cord (see pages 108–109), which may lead to paralysis or meningitis. More commonly, neck or lower back pain can be caused by muscle strain or damage to the ligaments or the disks between the vertebrae (the back bones). Broken ribs or damage to the muscles between the ribs at the back may also cause back pain.

TREATMENT

● Check the nature of the incident carefully— if the pain is related to a recent heavy fall or other accident, assume that there may be spinal cord damage and treat as for a broken back (see pages 108–109).

● Help the person to lie down. Usually the most comfortable position will be flat on the back on a hard surface.

<table>
<tr><td colspan="2" align="center">**SIGNS AND SYMPTOMS**</td></tr>
</table>

● Dull or severe pain, usually made worse by movement
● Tension in the neck or shoulders
● Pain travelling down limbs

● If the symptoms do not ease, seek medical attention promptly.

If back pain is accompanied by signs of spinal cord damage, such as numbness, tingling, or by headaches, nausea, vomiting, fever, or a deterioration in the level of consciousness (e.g. increasing drowsiness), call 911.

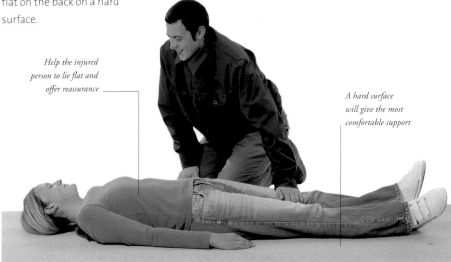

Help the injured person to lie flat and offer reassurance

A hard surface will give the most comfortable support

THE SPINE

The spine or backbone enables the body to stand upright, supports the head, and protects the spinal cord. Joints between vertebrae give the spine flexibility; ligaments and tendons stabilize the spine and control movement.

The spine is cushioned by shock-absorbing disks that lie between each vertebra.

Bony projections anchor ligaments and muscles, which stabilize the spine and control movement.

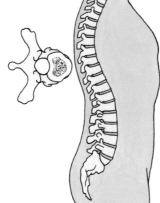

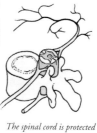

The spinal cord is protected by the bony spine, and spinal nerves pass through cavities in the vertebrae.

SIGNS AND SYMPTOMS OF SPINAL CORD DAMAGE

- Loss of movement below the site of the break
- Tingling in the fingers or toes or throughout the body
- Feeling strange, perhaps "jelly-like"
- Numbness

If any of these signs and symptoms is present, or if the nature of the accident indicates a potential fracture, assume that a bone is broken and keep the person still until help arrives.

WARNING

- **Do not give anything to eat or drink—the victim may need a general anesthetic in hospital.**
- **Do not move the victim unless he is in danger or requires resuscitation.**

If You Have to Move the Victim

The two key reasons for moving someone with a spinal injury are: to turn the person onto her back in order to resuscitate her; and to move her into the recovery position if she is unconscious and in a position that does not allow her to maintain a clear airway. For further information, see also Spinal Injury Recovery Position, pages 114–115.

NEUTRAL POSITION The best position for a person with a suspected neck or spinal injury is the neutral position. Here the head is in line with the neck and spine. To move a person into the neutral position, grip the head firmly over the ears and move it slowly into line. Once in this position, do not give up this support until medical help arrives to take over from you.

Only use this technique if you have been trained to do so.

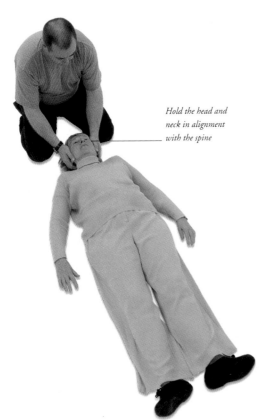

Hold the head and neck in alignment with the spine

LOG ROLL One of the most effective ways of turning a person over is the log roll technique. Log roll can also be used to turn somebody with a spinal injury onto her side as an alternative to the recovery position. It is also commonly used to move people with other injuries, such as a broken leg or pelvis, onto a stretcher or blanket.

Ideally, six people should be used to carry out this technique, with one person taking the lead and control of the head.

1 Place your hands over the ears with your fingers along the chin. Hold the head in the neutral position.

2 Ask the supporters to gently move the arms to the side of the body and to move the legs together.

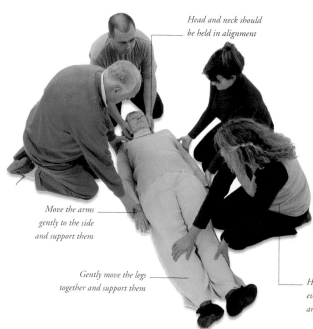

Head and neck should be held in alignment

Move the arms gently to the side and support them

Gently move the legs together and support them

Helpers should be evenly placed around the victim

Person at victim's head instructs other helpers

3 Ask the supporters to support the spine and limbs and to follow your commands.

4 Roll the victim like a log, keeping the head and chin in line with the neck and spine.

If you are by yourself and the injured person is not breathing, do not waste time searching for help. Turn the person as carefully as you can with any help available to you.

Helpers slowly roll victim onto her side

WHIPLASH

This is a common neck injury, particularly after car accidents. It accompanies a sudden impact accident when the person is wearing a seat belt and results from the head being thrown backward and forward violently. Whiplash is best described as a neck sprain. It is an injury to the soft tissue in the neck and can result in the need for long-term physcial therapy and the use of a neck collar. Whiplash may not appear until hours or even days after the injury.

It is very difficult to distinguish whiplash from spinal cord damage and a broken neck because the signs, symptoms, and potential causes are very similar and the pain of the whiplash injury may be masking other, more serious, problems. For this reason, whiplash should be treated in the same way as other spinal injuries until professional medical staff rule out more serious damage.

SPINAL INJURY RECOVERY POSITION

1 Support the victim's head as described on pages 112–113. Make yourself comfortable, because you will have to continue to do this until the ambulance arrives.

2 Ask a bystander to put the arm nearest the victim's shoulder gently underneath the victim's body, ensuring that the fingers are flat and the elbow straight. Bring the furthest arm across the body. The first responder must support the face.

3 The victim's furthest leg should be bent upward and the bystander's arm placed on the thigh just above the knee.

4 Working under orders from the first responder at the head, the victim should be gently turned, ensuring that the head, trunk, and toes stay in line.

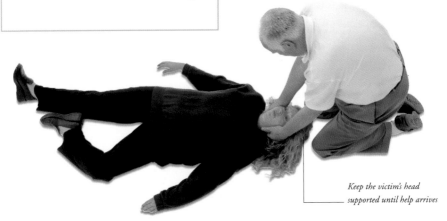

Keep the victim's head supported until help arrives

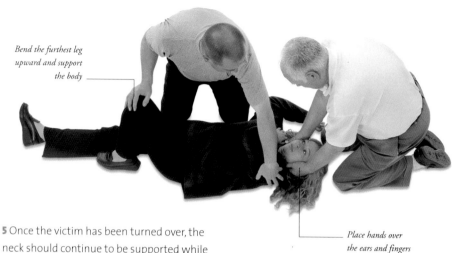

Bend the furthest leg upward and support the body

Place hands over the ears and fingers along the jaw

5 Once the victim has been turned over, the neck should continue to be supported while the bystander ensures that the victim is stable, either by supporting the body himself or by placing coats or rolled-up blankets, for example, around the victim.

Alternatively, you can use the log roll technique (see pages 112–113).

Turn the victim, keeping head, trunk, and toes in line

Let fluid drain from the mouth if necessary

Unconscious Victim

This is a particularly difficult situation to deal with. The victim's airway is always your first priority. The person may have a broken back that could cause nerve damage and paralysis, but if you do not protect the airway and ensure that the victim continues breathing, she will die.

TREATMENT If you come across an unconscious person for whom the nature of the accident or the positioning indicates that she may have broken her back (for example, a bystander tells you the victim fell, or the person is wearing motorcycle leathers and lying next to a damaged motorcycle), your priority remains to check the airway.

1 Ask a question to find out if the victim is conscious. Do not shake the victim.

2 Carry out your ABC checks (see pages 12–17), taking care to tilt the head gently. If the head is already extended a suitable way, do not move it any further. Instead, just use the chin lift and carefully check the mouth.

3 If the victim is not breathing, provide rescue breathing (see pages 24–28) and full CPR (see pages 29–33) as needed. Call 911 as soon as possible.

4 If you have to roll the victim onto her back to resuscitate, then you should aim to keep the victim's head, trunk, and toes in a straight line (see log roll, pages 112–113). If possible, get bystanders to help move the victim over, but do not waste time looking for help because the victim needs air as soon as possible.

5 If the victim is unconscious and lying in such a way that the head is extended and she is on her side, allowing fluid to drain from the mouth, then leave her alone.

6 Hold the victim's head still by placing your hands over the ears and your fingers along the jawline. Ensure that the airway is monitored.

7 If the victim is unconscious and either the head is not extended or she is not lying on her side, you need to move her into the recovery position. Ideally, with enough bystanders, you should use the log roll. If not, be prepared to roll the victim into the recovery position with all available help.

Injuries to the Lower Body

A broken bone in the lower body is a serious injury that requires hospital treatment. The pelvis is a large bone and is generally very difficult to break. Severe impact such as a fall from a height or a car accident are the most common cause in young, fit adults. In the elderly a broken pelvis (or hip) happens more often and can be caused by a relatively minor impact. In healthy adults it takes a major impact to break the thighbone and there are likely to be other injuries.

SIGNS AND SYMPTOMS OF A BROKEN PELVIS

- Bruising and swelling over the hip area
- Urge to urinate
- Blood-stained urine
- A sensation of falling apart: the pelvis is like a girdle and a break means that it may not be able to hold itself together
- Legs rotate outward as the support at the pelvis gives

Because the pelvis can also be broken at the back, it is easy to mistake a pelvic fracture for a spinal injury. If in doubt, treat for a broken spine (see pages 108–111).

BROKEN PELVIS The pelvis protects the urinary system and the biggest danger is that sharp bone ends may burst the bladder, creating the possibility of infection. Internal bleeding is another likelihood with a fractured hip, because the impact required to break the bone is likely to have caused other damage.

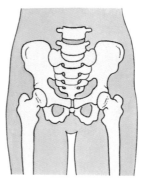

Left
A broken pelvis usually occurs as the result of a fall or a car accident. The main risk is of sharp bone ends puncturing the bladder, creating the risk of infection.

TREATMENT

1 Call an ambulance immediately and reassure the victim while you wait.

2 This is a very serious condition and it is best not to move the victim because you could easily make things worse.

3 If the ambulance will be some time, tie the legs gently together at the ankles and knees using triangular or improvised bandages.

4 Treat the victim for shock (see pages 44–45).

FRACTURES OF THE UPPER LEG The key risk with fractures of the femur (thigh bone) in the upper leg is shock. The thighbone protects the main artery in the leg, the femoral artery, and if broken may pierce it, causing severe internal bleeding.

A person with a broken thighbone will require transportation by ambulance. The general treatment is therefore nothing more than to immobilize the injured part and treat the victim for shock. Do not bandage the leg if help is on its way—this is likely to cause more pain and potentially cause further damage.

Support the leg above and below the site of the fracture if possible, placing padding around the broken leg to further help to reduce movement of the injured limb.

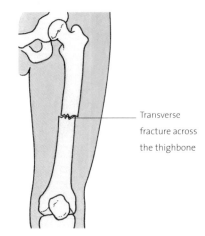

Transverse
fracture across
the thighbone

Above

A fractured thighbone may pierce the main artery in the leg, causing severe internal bleeding. The best treatment is to keep the limb still and treat the victim for shock.

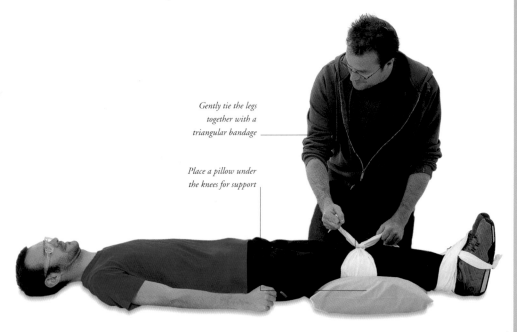

Gently tie the legs together with a triangular bandage

Place a pillow under the knees for support

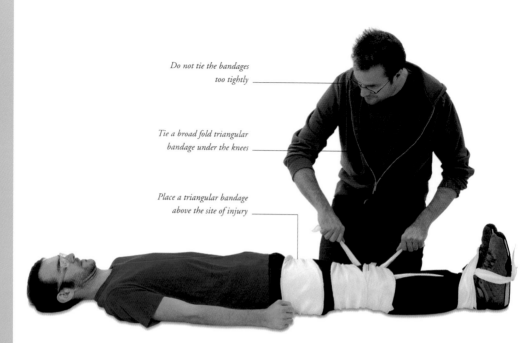

Do not tie the bandages too tightly

Tie a broad fold triangular bandage under the knees

Place a triangular bandage above the site of injury

If you have been trained in the use of traction then you may apply this gently to the leg to help to reduce pain and circulatory damage.

The injured person may benefit from immobilization of the broken leg by using the good leg as a splint, particularly if there will be a delay before medical help arrives.

1 Apply broad fold triangular bandages under the ankles, knees, and above and below the site of the fracture.

2 Place padding between the legs to help immobilize them.

3 Gently but firmly tie the bandages on the injured side.

4 Take care to check the circulation below the bandages to ensure that they do not become too tight as the leg swells.

WARNING
● **Do not give anything to eat or drink—the victim may need a general anesthetic in hospital.**
● **Do not move the victim unless he is in danger or needs resuscitation.**

Injuries to the Lower Leg

The long bones, the knee, and the foot are often injured during sports. There are two long bones in the lower leg. The tibia (shinbone) lies very close to the surface and if broken will often pierce the skin, causing an open fracture. The fibula lies behind the tibia. It is more difficult to break this bone and may not obviously affect the ability to walk. The knee is a complex joint vulnerable to fractures of the patella (kneecap), dislocation, strains, and cartilage (tissue) injury. It is unusual to break just one bone in the foot—generally, multiple fractures of the small bones in the foot and the toes are caused by crush injuries.

TREATING BROKEN LONG BONES

1 Help the injured person into the most comfortable position—generally, lying down.

2 Examine the injury carefully to see whether there is an open break. If there is a wound, cover gently with a sterile dressing or clean, non-fluffy material, pad around the broken area and tie gently but firmly into place.

Examine the leg gently to identify the injury

3 Gently support the injury above and below the site of the break. Place padding such as cushions or blankets around the site of the injury.

4 If you have been trained to do so, applying traction may help alleviate the pain and any potential damage to the circulation.

5 Treat for shock (see pages 44–45) and reassure.

TREATING A BROKEN LEG

A person with a broken leg is most likely to be transported to hospital by ambulance and the treatment in most settings is therefore limited to steady support and help with immobilization.

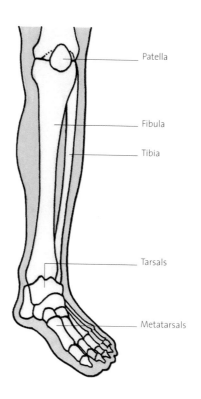

Patella

Fibula

Tibia

Tarsals

Metatarsals

Right
Lower leg bones are often injured during sport. The kneecap is particularly vulnerable to injury.

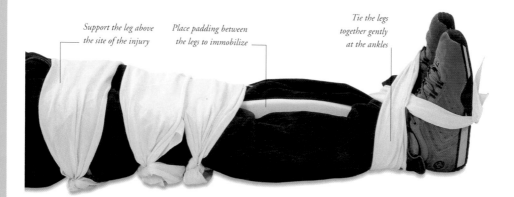

Support the leg above the site of the injury

Place padding between the legs to immobilize

Tie the legs together gently at the ankles

TREATING KNEE INJURIES In addition to the normal signs and symptoms of bone and soft tissue injuries, there may be an obvious displacement of the kneecap or an inability to bend or straighten the leg.

1 Help the injured person into the most comfortable position. He will generally need to be transported to hospital by ambulance.

2 Check the injured area carefully for an open break and treat as appropriate.

3 Pad around and under the injured area to provide support, gently tying the padding in place if needed.

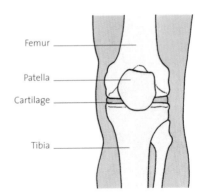

Femur

Patella

Cartilage

Tibia

Above
It may be difficult to identify a knee injury, and treatment for a damaged kneecap, sprains, and cartilage injury is broadly the same.

4 Treat for shock and reassure the victim until help arrives.

5 Do not try to bend the leg because you may cause more damage. Keep it still.

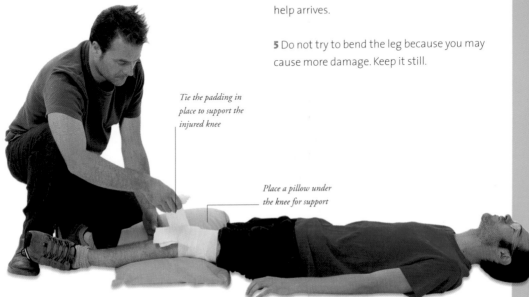

Tie the padding in place to support the injured knee

Place a pillow under the knee for support

TREATING A BROKEN FOOT

1 If possible, carefully remove the shoes and socks, tights, or stockings because the foot is likely to swell and these items of clothing may damage the circulation.

2 Cover any wound with a sterile dressing or clean, non-fluffy material.

3 Raise the foot to reduce swelling and pain and support with a large comfortable pad such as a cushion or blanket.

4 Wrap the foot in padding. If necessary, this can be held in place with a cover bandage (see Hand Fractures, page 105). A cold compress may further alleviate pain and swelling.

Take or send the injured person to hospital.

Above
A broken foot usually involves more than one fractured bone because it tends to be caused by a crush injury, when something heavy is dropped on it. Remove shoes and socks because the foot will probably swell and items of clothing may restrict circulation.

BONES OF THE FOOT

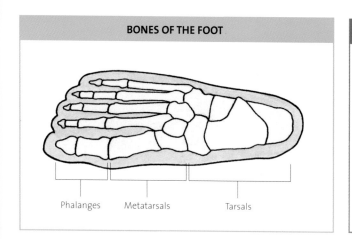

Phalanges   Metatarsals   Tarsals

WARNING

Do not give anything to eat or drink—the victim may need a general anesthetic in hospital.

Sprains and Strains

Strains occur when the muscle is overstretched, leading to a partial tear. Sprains are injuries to a ligament, a tough band of tissue that links two bones together at or near a joint. Commonly sprained joints include the wrist, knee, and ankle.

TREATMENT The person suffering the injury may often sense that the area is not broken—she may have suffered similar injuries before, particularly if the injury has occurred through sport. If both of you are confident that there is no other injury, then the best treatment is:

- Rest
- Ice
- Compression
- Elevation

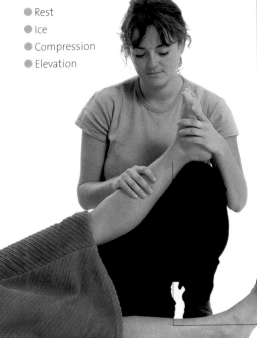

SIGNS AND SYMPTOMS

The signs and symptoms of strains, and more particularly sprains, are very similar to those of a broken bone. There may be pain, particularly on movement, swelling, and bruising (usually a little while after the accident). It is often impossible to tell if an injury is a sprain or a fracture without an X-ray and it is not unusual for sprains to take as long a time to heal as a simple break.

If in doubt, treat the injury as a broken bone and seek further medical help.

1 Place the injured part at rest. This prevents any further damage. Help the person into a comfortable position—for a leg injury, this will usually be lying down with head and shoulders supported.

Gently examine the site of injury to assess damage

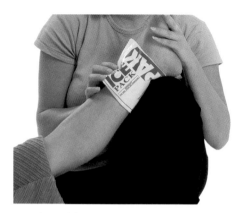

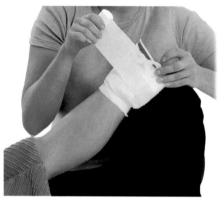

2 Apply a cold compress. Wrap some ice in a triangular bandage or other clean piece of material and hold gently on the site of the injury. This will help relieve pain and reduce swelling. Do not apply ice directly to the injury because this may damage the skin. Cool the injury for 10–15 minutes, keeping the compress cold with refills as necessary.

3 Apply a compressing gauze wrap. This will help reduce pain and swelling and will provide support for the injury.

ALTERNATIVE COLD COMPRESSES

If ice is not readily available, soak a flannel or other piece of material in very cold water, wring it out, and apply to the injury. Replace this every 2–3 minutes as the material warms up. Alternatively, consider the contents of the freezer. Frozen peas make an excellent cold compress as the bag conforms to the shape of the injury.

4 Elevate the injured part. Elevation will help reduce swelling and pain. If the arm is injured, use either the other arm or elevation sling as appropriate to provide additional support.

5 Seek medical assistance and make sure the victim keeps the limb raised and supported until help arrives.

Burns and Scalds

Burns and scalds, a type of burn caused by wet heat, are potentially fatal injuries. They can cause life-threatening shock through serious fluid loss and, if around the face and neck, can restrict breathing.

WHAT ARE THE RISKS FROM BURNS? In burns, fluid is lost in three main ways:

- Blistering
- Swelling around the injury
- Directly from the injury

While the fluid loss may not be visible as liquid lying around the victim it is nevertheless lost from the blood as a straw-colored substance known as plasma. Severe burns therefore can and often do prove to be fatal.

The second risk from burns is infection. The damaged tissue provides little or no resistance to infection and serious problems may arise some time after the initial injury. The risk of infection increases with the size and depth of the burn, and the victim will probably suffer from shock as well.

CAUSES OF BURNS

Dry heat This is the most common type of burn and includes burns caused by hot objects such as exhausts or by cigarettes or lighters.

Wet heat Also known as a scald, wet heat usually refers to hot water or steam but it can also include other hot liquids such as oil or fat.

Friction When two objects rub together very quickly friction generates heat, causing another kind of dry burn.

Chemical burns Industrial and household chemicals can cause serious burns.

Electrical burns These can be caused by the everyday low-voltage currents found in switches, wires, and appliances around the home or from the high-voltage cables scattered around the countryside in the form of power lines, subway tracks, and so forth. In rarer cases electrical burns can be caused by lightning strikes.

Radiation burns While this may sound dramatic, most of us have suffered some degree of radiation burn at some point in our lives—more commonly known as as sunburn.

DEPTH OF THE BURN

Burns are classified into three types:

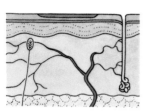 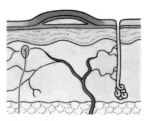 

First degree burns involve only the outer layer of skin and, although often extremely painful, are generally not life-threatening unless a very large surface area of the body is covered. The burned area is very sore and is usually red and possibly a little swollen. If good first aid treatment is applied and the area burned is not extensive, then further medical treatment is unlikely to be needed.

Second degree burns include the top layers of skin and involve blistering. They are characterized by red, raw-looking skin, blisters that weep clear fluid, and pain. The risk of shock (see pages 44–45) is high with second degree burns and any burn of this type needs medical attention. Second degree burns covering a substantial percentage of the body can kill.

Third degree burns involve damage to all the layers of skin, usually including the nerve endings and other underlying tissues and organs. Characterized by charred tissue often surrounded by white waxy areas of dead skin with damaged nerves, third degree burns will always need emergency medical attention and in the long term will often require plastic surgery.

AREA OF THE BODY BURNED Generally, the larger the area of the body burned, the more serious the burn. Any burn to the face or neck needs urgent medical attention. As a general principle, if the victim has other injuries, appears to be in a great deal of pain, is showing signs and symptoms of shock, is having difficulty breathing, or you have other reasons to suspect that his or her condition is more serious, then call an ambulance whatever the extent or depth of the burn.

HOW DO YOU TELL HOW SEVERE A BURN IS?

Many burns are minor and can be safely treated at home or with help from a local doctor or pharmacist.

However, the size and depth of the burn will tell you if it needs urgent medical treatment.

How to Treat Burns and Scalds

The general treatment of all burns is very simple: cool and cover the affected part, and seek appropriate medical help. Before you do anything else, make sure that you protect yourself. This is particularly important at accident scenes. Ensure that the fire is out, any electrical equipment is safely disconnected, and that any chemical spills are not going to affect you.

TREATMENT

1 Monitor the victim's airway and breathing (see pages 12–15). This is particularly important if the victim has burns to the mouth and airway. Be prepared to resuscitate if necessary (see pages 29–33).

2 If possible lay the victim on the ground to help reduce the effects of shock.

3 Douse the burned area with cool liquid. Cooling the burn will reduce the pain, swelling, and risk of scarring. Restrict the cool liquid to the injured part wherever possible because over-cooling could lead to hypothermia, particularly if the surrounding air temperature is low. If applying water from a shower, hose, or tap, ensure that the pressure is minimal because water hitting burned skin at speed will add to the pain and the damage.

4 Make an assessment about whether or not an ambulance is needed and call for help. If in doubt, call 911.

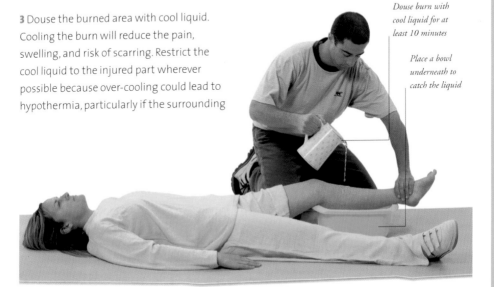

Douse burn with cool liquid for at least 10 minutes

Place a bowl underneath to catch the liquid

5 Keep cooling the injured part until the pain stops. Often 10 minutes is sufficient but if the victim still complains of pain after this time then continue with the cooling treatment.

6 Remove rings, watches, and other potential constricting items as burns swell up. Take care to return these items to the casualty.

7 Once the pain has eased, cover the wound to prevent infection. This should be done with a sterile bandage if possible, tied very loosely over the burn. If in any doubt as to whether material may stick to the wound, do not attempt to cover but continue to cool the burns continuously until medical help arrives. If you are having to improvise, any clean, non-fluffy material can be used—ideal examples are clean handkerchiefs, cotton pillowcases, or plastic wrap.

8 If possible, raise the injured part as this can help to reduce swelling.

Stay with the injured person until help arrives or, if the burn is less serious, accompany her to further medical attention.

● Continue to treat for shock.
● Maintain a check on the victim's airway, breathing, and circulation.
● Keep checking bandages to ensure that they are not too tight.

WARNING

● Do not over-cool the victim.
● Do not apply water under pressure.
● Do not remove burned clothing if it is sticking to the wound.
● Do not put cotton wool or any other fluffy material on to a burn as it will stick to the injury.
● Do not put any creams or ointments on to a burn because these will need to be removed at the hospital.
● Do not burst blisters because this may increase the risk of infection.

SUMMARY

1 Check for danger
2 Assess ABC (be prepared to resuscitate if necessary)
3 Cool the injured part
4 Make an appropriate decision about what help is required and call for an ambulance if necessary
5 Cover the injured part
6 Treat for shock throughout your treatment of the burn
7 Elevate the injured part if possible

Treating other Types of Burn

The general principle of treating burns remains to cool and cover the affected area but some types of burn need extra consideration. With burns to the neck and mouth, beyond the risk of shock and infection, the greatest potential problem is the risk of airway obstruction due to swelling. The obvious additional danger with electrical burns is the combination of water as a treatment and electricity as the cause.

**TREATING BURNS
TO THE NECK AND MOUTH**

1 Check the victim's airway and breathing and be prepared to resuscitate if necessary (see pages 29–33).

2 Call an ambulance and reassure the victim until help arrives.

Remove clothing if it is not stuck to the burn

3 Get the victim into a position where his breathing is comfortable (this will usually be sitting up).

4 Loosen any constriction around the neck to ease breathing. Keep the airway clear.

5 Cool any burns continuously—do not attempt to cover.

6 Maintain a check on the victim's airway and breathing (see pages 12–15).

Douse the burn with cool liquid and do not cover

LIGHTNING

Although rare, lightning strikes do happen and can kill. If caught outside in a thunderstorm, seek shelter in a car or building.

If there is no shelter, make yourself as low as possible, minimize your contact with the ground by crouching and avoid single trees, bodies of water, and tall objects.

If a person has been struck by lightning, check their airway and breathing, be prepared to resuscitate, treat any burns, and call for help.

ELECTRICAL BURNS If a victim has suffered from an electric shock, do not attempt to touch the person unless you are absolutely certain that he or she is no longer in contact with live equipment. If the person is still attached to an electrical current, your best option is to turn the electricity off at the main breaker. If you cannot access the breaker, you may be able to turn off electrical equipment at the wall socket but be particularly careful that you do not touch the victim or any live equipment.

If there is no way to turn the electricity off, you can attempt to move the victim away from the point of contact using a non-conducting material such as a broom handle. Be sure to insulate yourself as much as possible by wearing rubber gloves and shoes, and by standing on a telephone directory.

Electricity demands respect—if in doubt, call in professional help. Do not put yourself in any danger.

TREATING ELECTRICAL BURNS

A victim suffering from an electrical burn may well have respiratory or circulatory difficulties. An electrical discharge across the heart can make the heart stop beating (see Heart Attack, pages 53–55), so be prepared to resuscitate the victim over and above the treatment of any burn that may be present.

1 Make absolutely sure that there is no further risk from the electricity.

2 Check to see whether the victim is conscious. If unconscious, check airway and breathing and take action as appropriate.

HIGH-VOLTAGE ELECTRICITY

High-voltage electricity (power lines, subway tracks, overhead power cables, etc.) usually kills immediately, causing severe burns, heart problems, and potentially even broken bones and internal injuries as the victim is thrown by the shock. If somebody has been hit, your first priority is to keep yourself and other bystanders safe. High-voltage currents can jump some distance so keep people back at least 60 feet and call for professional help via 911.

3 Treat any burns with cold water if safe to do so.

4 Cover burns as appropriate with sterile, non-fluffy dressings.

5 Seek urgent medical attention. Stay with the victim and reassure him until medical help arrives.

Use a broom to move a power tool away from a victim

Chemical Burns and Eye Burns

While the general rules for the treatment of burns are the same, regardless of the type of burn, there are some additional considerations for chemical burns. The key point when dealing with chemicals is not to contaminate yourself. Chemical spills are not always obvious—some very toxic chemicals look like water—so look for signs such as a HAZMAT (hazardous material) label, empty chemical containers, or guidance from bystanders. If in doubt, call 911 rather than approach the injured person yourself. Remember that some household substances, particularly cleaning materials such as oven cleaner, can cause chemical burns.

TREATING CHEMICAL BURNS

1 If you feel that you can safely approach the victim, then do so carefully.

2 If necessary, wear protective clothing to protect yourself from contamination.

3 Ventilate the room if possible because many chemicals affect breathing.

4 When cooling the burn with water, ensure that the contaminated water drains away from both the victim and yourself. It may be necessary to flood the injured part for longer to ensure that the chemical is totally washed away. This may take more than 20 minutes.

5 Call 911. Make sure you have mentioned that it is a chemical burn so that additional help can be sent for if necessary and so that any antidotes can be sent with the ambulance.

6 If possible, remove contaminated clothes from the victim because these may keep burning, but only do this if you can do it without contaminating yourself or causing the victim more harm.

7 Cover the burn with a clean, non-fluffy material as appropriate and tie loosely in place if necessary.

8 Treat for shock (see pages 44–45) and reassure the victim until emergency help arrives on the scene.

WHAT IF THE CHEMICAL REACTS WITH WATER?

Some industrial chemicals do react badly with water. Where such chemicals are used, people working with them should have been trained in the use of an antidote. If there is nobody around with this expertise, do not waste time looking for an antidote—apply liberal amounts of water to try to wash the chemical away.

CHEMICAL BURNS TO THE EYE Chemical burns to the eye can be very serious. Early rinsing of the eye with cold water will help to flush away the chemical and reduce scarring.

TREATMENT

1 Protect yourself, the victim, and bystanders from further contamination.

2 Hold the affected eye under cold running water for at least 10 minutes to flush out the chemical, allowing the injured person to blink periodically. You may need to hold the eyelid open. Make sure that the water flow is gentle. Do not allow contaminated water to fall across the good eye and so contaminate that eye also.

3 Ask the injured person to hold a non-fluffy sterile or clean pad across the eye, tying it in place if hospital treatment may be delayed.

4 Take or send the person to hospital with details of the chemical if possible.

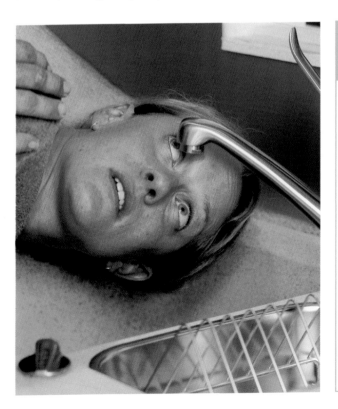

SIGNS AND SYMPTOMS OF CHEMICAL BURNS TO THE EYE

- Known exposure to chemical
- Intense pain
- Redness and swelling
- Reluctance or inability to open the eye
- Tears from eye

FLASH BURNS TO THE EYE Caused by looking into very bright light, flash burns damage the surface of the cornea, the transparent front of the eyeball. Recovery can take some time and in some instances the damage can be permanent (for example, if a person has looked at the sun through a telescope without appropriate protection).

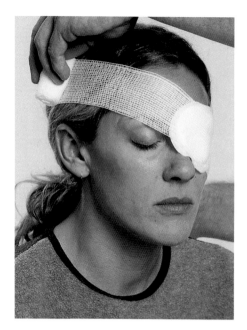

TREATMENT

1 Check the history to rule out chemical burns or a foreign body in the eye.

2 Reassure the injured person, and wear gloves to prevent infecting the eye.

SIGNS AND SYMPTOMS OF FLASH BURNS TO THE EYE

- Known exposure to intense light (which may have happened some time ago)
- Intense pain
- Feeling that there may be something in the eyes
- Redness and watering
- Both eyes affected

CONTACT LENSES

Where there has been any injury to the eye, encourage the injured person to leave contact lenses in place.

3 Place pads over both eyes and bandage in place if it will be some time until medical help arrives. Remember that this will effectively blind the person temporarily so stay with her to reassure and guide.

4 Take or send the person to hospital because she will need medical attention.

Extreme Cold

Hypothermia, a condition that occurs when the body temperature falls below the normal range, is caused by a low surrounding temperature and can lead to death. Freezing temperatures cause frostbite, whereby ice forms in the body tissue and destroys it. The risk of frostbite is increased by windy conditions.

CAUSES OF HYPOTHERMIA Hypothermia (low temperature) occurs when the body temperature falls below the normal range, and can lead to death. The average temperature of a healthy adult is 96.8–100.4°F. Hypothermia occurs when the body's core temperature falls below 95°F. Survival is unlikely, but not unheard of, below 79°F.

There are a number of factors that heighten the risk of becoming hypothermic. These include:

● Age
The elderly are at greater risk from hypothermia: low mobility combined with poor circulation, a reduced sensitivity to the cold, and a greater potential for slips and falls means that an elderly person may develop hypothermia in temperatures that a healthy younger adult could tolerate.

The very young are also at an increased risk because the mechanisms for controlling their own body temperature are poorly developed. They may look healthy but their skin will feel cold and their behavior may be abnormally quiet or listless.

● Exposure to wind or rain
● Immersion in cold water
● Lack of food
● Alcohol and drugs

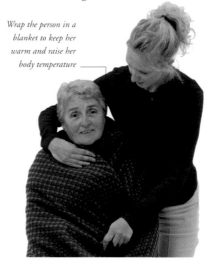

Wrap the person in a blanket to keep her warm and raise her body temperature

Right
If a person is suffering from hypothermia, replace damp clothing if necessary, wrap up well, and give high energy foods and hot drinks to restore body temperature to normal.

SIGNS AND SYMPTOMS
OF HYPOTHERMIA

Early signs:
- Shivering
- Pale, cold skin
- Cold environment
- Presence of an increased risk factor as listed left

As the condition gets worse:
- No shivering, even though the person is cold
- Increasing drowsiness
- Irrational behavior and confusion
- Slow, shallow breathing
- Slow, weak pulse

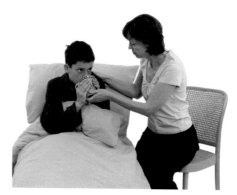

Above

Keep the person warm and provide with high energy foods and warm drinks.

TREATMENT

If the person is unconscious

Open the airway and check for breathing (see pages 12–17). Be prepared to resuscitate if necessary (see pages 29–33). Hypothermia slows the body's functions down before stopping the heart, and it is therefore not uncommon to hear of people with hypothermia being successfully resuscitated some time after the heart has stopped.

If the person is conscious

1 Improve the surroundings. If the person is outdoors, bring them in or take them to shelter. If the person is indoors, warm the room but do not overheat (77°F).

2 Replace wet clothes with dry warm clothing if possible.

3 A healthy adult may be best rewarmed by soaking in a warm bath of 104°F. Do not use this technique on an elderly person or a child.

4 Wrap the person up and give high energy foods and warm drinks. Remember that heat is lost through the extremities so cover the head, hands, and feet.

5 Check for other conditions or injuries that may have occured. The confusion caused by hypothermia may mask other signs and symptoms. If there is no improvement, or the level of consciousness deteriorates, seek medical advice. For young children and the elderly, who are particularly vulnerable, always seek medical attention if you suspect hypothermia. Warm them slowly.

FROSTBITE

Frostbite occurs in freezing conditions and is the freezing of body tissue at the extremities, most commonly the fingers, toes, and earlobes. If it is not treated early enough it can lead to gangrene and to amputation. Frostbitten skin is highly susceptible to infection.

Treatment

1 Remove tight items such as rings and watches that may further damage circulation. Warm the injured part slowly by holding it.

2 Get the person to shelter. Do not attempt to thaw the injured part if it is liable to be re-exposed to cold, because this will do more damage.

3 Handle the injured part carefully because the tissue is very fragile and may be easily damaged. Do not apply direct heat, rub, or allow the injured person to apply pressure to (for example, do not let the person walk if the toes are affected). Place the injured part in warm water if available. Otherwise continue warming the unjured part with your hand.

4 Pat dry and then cover with a light gauze bandage. Remember that the injured part will be exceptionally painful for the victim.

5 Raise the injured part to help alleviate pain and swelling and allow the injured person to take acetaminophen if able to.

6 Watch for hypothermia and treat as appropriate.

7 Seek medical attention, particularly if the site of the freezing does not regain a healthy color or is black.

SIGNS AND SYMPTOMS OF FROSTBITE

● Freezing environment

Early signs
● Tingling
● Pale skin

As the condition gets worse
● Numbness
● Hardening of the skin
● Skin color changes to white through blue and finally black

When thawed, the injured part is extremely painful and there may be blistering of the skin.

Extreme Heat

Heat exhaustion is a condition resulting from the loss of fluid and salt, usually through excessive sweating. Heatstroke generally occurs rapidly when the brain's temperature regulator fails to work effectively. This tends to occur when a person has been in a very hot environment or has a fever caused by a condition such as malaria.

HEAT EXHAUSTION Heat exhaustion is very similar to shock (see pages 44–45) in that fluid is being lost from the body. It most commonly occurs when a person has been exercising and not replacing fluid content: cyclists and joggers are common sufferers from the condition.

TREATMENT

1 Lay the victim down in a cool place and raise her legs.

2 If the victim is conscious give sips of a weak salt solution (one teaspoon to one litre of water).

3 Maintain a check on the victim's consciousness level (see pages 61–63). If it deteriorates, place the victim in the recovery position (see pages 20–23) and call for emergency assistance.

4 If the victim's condition improves rapidly, advise her to see a doctor.

SIGNS AND SYMPTOMS OF HEAT EXHAUSTION

- History of exertion
- Pale, cold, and clammy skin
- Fast, weak pulse
- Fast, shallow breathing
- Nausea
- Dizziness and disorientation
- Lapse into unconsciousness

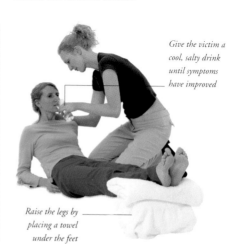

Give the victim a cool, salty drink until symptoms have improved

Raise the legs by placing a towel under the feet

HEATSTROKE In heatstroke, the body becomes very hot very quickly and this condition can be fatal. The signs and symptoms are very similar to those of a stroke (see pages 56–57).

TREATMENT

1 Check airway and breathing (see pages 12–17). If unconscious, turn the victim into the recovery position (see pages 20–23). Be prepared to resuscitate if necessary (see pages 29–33).

2 If the victim is conscious, move to a cool environment. If this is impossible or the victim is unconscious, try to cool the environment (use fans, open doors, and keep crowds away).

3 Call for emergency assistance and reassure the victim if he or she is conscious.

4 Remove outer clothes and wrap the victim in a cold, wet sheet. Keep it wet. Continue the cooling process. If the body temperature drops, replace the wet sheet with a dry one.

5 Continue to monitor the victim while you wait for help.

SIGNS AND SYMPTOMS

- Hot, flushed, and dry skin
- Slow, full, and bounding pulse
- Noisy breathing
- High body temperature
- Headache
- Disorientation
- Lapse into unconsciousness

SLIP SLAP SLOP

The three simple rules for prevention of sun-related problems are:

Slip into a T-shirt
Slap on a hat
Slop on the suncream

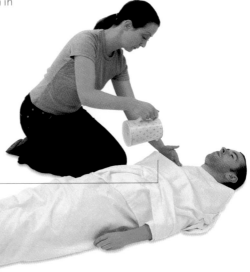

Wrap the victim in a sheet and keep this wet to reduce heatstroke

Poisoning

A poison is any substance that enters the body and causes temporary or permanent harm.

Some substances, such as acetaminophen or alcohol, only become harmful to the body when

taken in a large quantity. Others, such as some herbicides, need only to be taken in very small

amounts to be harmful.

HOW DO POISONS AFFECT THE BODY?

Different poisons have different effects. The effect is modified by the quantity and the time since exposure.

POTENTIAL EFFECTS OF POISONS

Vomiting This is a common response to many poisons, particularly those that have been eaten, as the body tries to remove the poison from the system.

Impaired consciousness A person may be confused and slowly lapse into full unconsciousness.

Breathing difficulties Poison may eventually cause breathing to stop.

Change in heart rate Some poisons speed up the heart rate; others slow it down. Poisons may eventually cause the heart to stop.

Erratic and confused behavior Always suspect poisoning in these instances.

Burns Some poisons burn the skin, some swallowed poisons burn the digestive tract, bringing the additional risk of swelling around the mouth and throat.

Pain Some poisons will cause pain.

Liver and kidney problems As the liver and kidneys struggle to remove poisons from the body they may become affected themselves.

Vomiting is the body's way of removing poisons from the system

KEY FIRST AID PRINCIPLES
FOR DEALING WITH POISONS

1 Protect yourself and bystanders from the source of the poison by making the scene safe and wearing protective clothing if necessary.

2 Monitor and maintain the victim's airway and breathing (see pages 12–17) and be prepared to resuscitate if necessary (see pages 29–33).

3 Seek appropriate medical help or call the Poison Control Hotline to deal with dangerous substances.

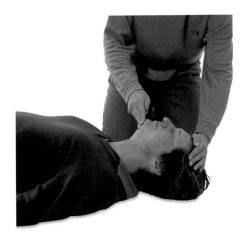

4 Monitor the victim's level of consciousness and be prepared to turn into the recovery position (see pages 20–23) if necessary.

5 Support the victim if he vomits and place in the recovery position until medical help arrives.

6 Treat any burns caused by corrosive poisons by flooding the affected area with running water (see Chemical Burns, pages 133–135).

7 Try to identify the source of the poison because this will help determine appropriate medical treatment.

THERE ARE FOUR KEY WAYS IN WHICH POISONS CAN ENTER THE BODY

Method	Examples
Eating (ingestion)	Foods carrying bacteria that cause food poisoning
	Prescription drugs taken as a deliberate or accidental overdose
	Alcohol in excess
	Household chemicals (children particularly are prone to drinking from chemical containers while playing)
	Plants (for example, magic mushrooms may be eaten deliberately when seeking an effect, or by accident)
Breathing in (inhalation)	Carbon monoxide (in exhaust fumes)
	Fumes in house fires
Injection	Prescription drugs taken as a deliberate or accidental overdose
	Illegal drugs
	Insect bites and stings
Through the skin (absorption)	Many industrial chemicals
	Herbicides

CLUES TO IDENTIFYING POISONS

The early identification of a poison will help medical staff determine an appropriate course of treatment. Potential clues that you as the first person at the scene of the incident may be able to provide include:

● Medicine bottles/pill containers (do not assume that an empty bottle means that all the pills were taken).
● Samples of vomit: if the victim is sick, keep the vomit for inspection.

● Details of what happened from bystanders or from the victim.
● Identification of animal or insect: if the poisoning route was a bite, try to get a description of the creature. If it is safe to do so, take the poisonous animal or insect to hospital.
● Chemical containers: be able to describe any HAZMAT symbol or label if you can get close enough to do so without putting yourself at risk. Do not touch these yourself. Remember that many household substances are toxic.

Poisoning from Household Chemicals

Many everyday household substances are potentially poisonous if misused. Unfortunately, many hospital admissions are the result of children drinking household chemicals while playing. Inside the home, cleaning materials are often the biggest risk, while in the garden herbicides, pesticides, and paint stripper are common culprits. Most household chemicals cause problems when they are swallowed. Many are corrosive and together with the effect of the poison may also cause burns to the mouth and food canal (digestive tract).

MANAGING SWALLOWED POISONS

TREATMENT

Make sure that it is safe for you to approach. Do not inadvertently kneel in chemicals or otherwise expose yourself to any risk.

1 Monitor and maintain the airway and breathing (see pages 12–17). Be prepared to resuscitate (see pages 29–33) if necessary.

2 Monitor consciousness. If the person becomes unconscious, put into the recovery position (see pages 20–23).

3 Call 911 or the Poison Control Hotline for advice on how to proceed.

4 Treat any burns (see pages 126–135), wearing protective clothing if necessary.

5 Support the person if he vomits and place in the recovery position if necessary.

6 Reassure the person while you are waiting for emergency assistance to arrive.

7 Identify the poison if possible because this will help medical staff determine what treatment is appropriate.

SIGNS AND SYMPTOMS

- Signs of bottles, information from the victim, or from bystanders
- Burns to the mouth
- Vomiting
- Pain
- Impaired consciousness
- Difficulty breathing

IF THERE ARE MOUTH BURNS If the person
stops breathing you will need to provide
rescue breathing (see pages 24–28). However,
if there are mouth burns because the poison
was corrosive, you must take care not to put
yourself at risk. Use a face shield or mask while
rescue breathing. This should be placed over
the victim's face and the oval tube placed
between the teeth. The plastic shield forms
a barrier as you give mouth-to-mouth.

If there is no shield available, consider
providing rescue breathing mouth-to-nose.
Tilt the head and lift the chin as you would

normally. Then close the mouth (using a piece
of material as a barrier against the poison if
appropriate) and seal your mouth around the
victim's nose. Provide rescue breathing at the
same rate and ratio as you would when giving
mouth-to-mouth. Take your mouth away after
each breath and open the victim's mouth
between breaths to let the air out.

If the victim is breathing and conscious, you
may provide relief from the burning by giving
frequent sips of cold water. This will help
relieve pain and reduce swelling.

Above
*You will need to give
mouth-to-mouth
resuscitation if a person stops
breathing but if there are
burns to the mouth you
must use a face shield or
mask to protect yourself.*

Above
*Place the plastic face shield
or mask over the victim's face
and place the oval tube
between the teeth. The
shield forms a barrier as
you provide rescue breathing.*

**PREVENTION OF POISONING
FROM HOUSEHOLD SUBSTANCES**

● Put all household cleaning materials
and medicines up high out of the reach
of children
● Consider putting any dangerous
substances in a locked cupboard
● Always read instructions for use carefully.
Some household chemicals should be used
only in a well-ventilated room or with some
protective clothing
● Always store chemicals in the container
they came in or a clearly marked alternative.
Never store chemicals in drinks containers
or unmarked bottles
● Keep gardening supplies securely in the
shed or garage in a locked container
● Where possible, buy medicines and
cleaning materials in childproof containers

Poisoning from Industrial Chemicals

The use of hazardous industrial chemicals is strictly controlled and regulated, and those who work with such substances are aware of the specific first aid and safety requirements. For most people, contact with dangerous industrial chemicals will be through a chemical spill at a road accident or a problem at an engineering plant.

TREATMENT Many industrial chemicals can be absorbed through the skin or inhaled, so it is important not to approach an accident scene unless you are sure you can do so safely. If you are at all unsure of the risk, do not approach the scene. Instead, call 911 immediately, giving as much information about the incident as you can. Encourage victims who can to move away from the source of any danger.

Inhaled poisons Where possible, remove the victim from the chemical. If this is not possible, ensure that the area is well-ventilated (open doors and windows). If in doubt, do not stay in the room yourself. Many chemicals have no odour or obvious effect and you may not be aware that you are being poisoned.

1 Monitor and maintain the victim's airway and breathing (see pages 12–17) and be prepared to resuscitate if necessary (see pages 29–33).

2 If the victim becomes unconscious, place in the recovery position (see pages 20–23).

3 If the victim is conscious, help into the most comfortable position. If there are breathing problems, this position is most likely to be sitting up.

4 Call 911 and provide as much information as you can.

Poisons on the skin

1 Do not contaminate yourself. Wear protective clothing if available.

2 Wash away the chemical with water, taking care to flush the contaminated water away from both yourself and the victim.

3 Monitor and maintain the victim's airway and breathing and be prepared to resuscitate if necessary.

4 Call 911 and reassure the victim until help arrives.

Drug Poisoning

Drug poisoning can be deliberate or accidental. Drugs may be prescription only, illegally supplied, or freely available from a chemist. Signs and symptoms of drug poisoning will vary, depending on the drug that has been taken.

TREATMENT

1 Keep yourself safe. The effect of some drugs, both legally and illegally supplied, can be to cause aggression or irrational behavior in the person who has taken them. If this is the case, do not approach the victim. Call 911 instead and explain the situation. They will make a decision about whether the police need to be called.

2 Monitor and maintain the airway and breathing (see pages 12–17) and be prepared to resuscitate (see pages 29–33) if necessary, if it is safe for you to do so.

3 If the person becomes unconscious, place him or her into the recovery position (see pages 20–23).

4 Call 911 and stay by the victim until assistance arrives.

5 Look for clues as to the cause of the poisoning and inform medical staff.

Above
Do not assume that an empty container means all the drugs have been taken, but do pass it on to medical staff.

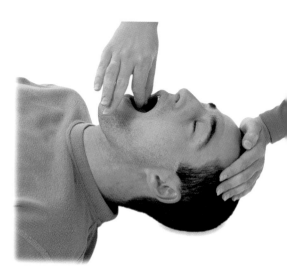

Right
Monitor and maintain the airway and breathing, clearing any obstructions that are in the mouth.

COMMON TYPES OF DRUGS AND THEIR EFFECTS

Analgesics (painkillers)

Opioids (derived from opium, e.g. morphine, diamorphine (heroin)) — Act on the brain and spinal cord to stop the perception of pain. Produce a state of well-being and relaxation. While they have legitimate medical use, they are among the most commonly abused drugs. Side effects include nausea, vomiting, constricted pupils, constipation, and slow and shallow breathing. Overdose may lead to unconsciousness and death.

Non-opioids (e.g. acetaminophen) — Act in a similar way to the opioids but with fewer side effects. Signs of an overdose may not be immediately obvious but if the antidote is not administered swiftly, fatal liver failure can set in, even in an adult who appears to be healthy. Signs include pain, nausea, and vomiting.

NSAIDs Non-steroidal anti-inflammatories (e.g. aspirin, ibuprofen) — Act at the site of pain to prevent the painful stimulation of nerve endings. While generally safe, they can irritate the stomach lining, causing pain and bleeding, particularly in those susceptible to stomach ulcers.

Sleeping drugs and antidepressants

Benzodiazepines and barbiturates — Act by depressing brain function. Minor side effects include slow mental activity and drowsiness. Effects of overdose include gradual decline into unconsciousness, shallow breathing, and abnormal pulse rate.

Stimulants and hallucinogens

Amphetamines (e.g. speed) — Act by stimulating the central nervous system (the brain and spinal cord). Signs include out-of-character behavior, hallucinations, energetic sweating, and increased heart rate.

Alcohol Poisoning

Alcohol depresses the central nervous system, which is the centre of our thoughts, feelings, and senses, and is responsible for coordinating all movement and body processes. In the early stages of drinking, this creates a relaxed feeling and impression of increased confidence. Continued drinking can affect the ability to make rational decisions and, as consumption increases, will slow down breathing and can even cause loss of consciousness. The effect of alcohol on the body is affected by factors including weight, body fat, and history of alcohol intake. What may be a safe level for one person may have serious effects for another.

EFFECTS OF HIGH INTAKE There are four key risks following a high alcohol intake:

- Injury, as a result poor decision-making and clumsiness.
- Vomiting, leading to choking in an unconscious person.
- Hypothermia—caused by alcohol dilating the blood vessels, making exposure to the cold a greater risk.
- Slower breathing and, ultimately, breathing stopping.

Right
Be prepared to resuscitate if necessary. If the victim becomes unconscious, place in the recovery position.

TREATMENT

1 Monitor and maintain the person's airway and breathing (see pages 12–17). Be prepared to resuscitate the person (see pages 29–33) if necessary.

2 If the person becomes unconscious, place into the recovery position (see pages 20–23). The person is extremely likely to vomit, so watch carefully for signs of vomit and remove from the mouth as needed.

3 If the person is conscious, help into a comfortable position and encourage him or her to keep still.

4 Check for additional injury and give treatment as appropriate.

5 Protect from extremes of cold to reduce the risk of hypothermia developing. If the person is unconscious, you suspect further injury, you are worried that other substances may have been consumed, or you have any other doubts as to their condition, call 911. Do not underestimate the risk of alcohol poisoning.

SIGNS AND SYMPTOMS

● What has happened. Consider this carefully—a person who has suffered a head injury or stroke may show similar signs and symptoms to somebody who is drunk

● Strong smell of alcohol

● Lapsing in and out of consciousness. Rousable at first but eventually slipping into full unconsciousness

● Red, sweating face

● Deep, noisy breathing—sounds of snoring

● Strong, fast pulse

Eventually, breathing may become shallower and the pulse weaker and faster.

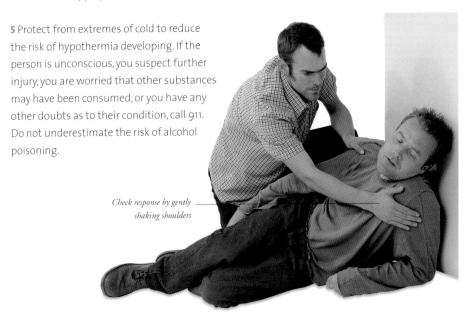

Check response by gently shaking shoulders

If you do not feel that an ambulance is necessary, ensure that the person is not left alone, that the airway and breathing are regularly checked, and that the victim is in a safe, warm place until he is better.

Place in recovery position if unconscious

Keep warm to lessen risk of hypothermia

LONG-TERM EFFECTS OF ALCOHOL

Drinking alcohol within safe limits may be beneficial for health, helping to protect against stroke and heart disease, but if you have more than a couple of alcoholic drinks a day, there are more risks than benefits.

● Weight gain: alcohol contains many calories and regular drinkers often put on weight.

● Reduced intellectual function: brain cells that control memory and learning are damaged by alcohol. Alcohol is damaging to mental health, causing increased anxiety and depression.

● Increased risk of developing many types of cancer (this risk is even higher if you smoke as well).

● Increased risk of circulatory disorders such as high blood pressure and stroke.

● Reduced fertility in both men and women and damage to the fetus if you drink heavily during pregnancy.

● Damage to the liver and other organs; digestive problems such as ulcers.

Food Poisoning

There are several forms of food poisoning. Bacterial food poisoning is often caused by bacteria in food that has been poorly prepared. Salmonella is one of the most common culprits and is found in many farm products such as eggs and chickens. Toxic (potentially lethal) food poisoning such as botulism can be due to poisons caused by bacteria in certain types of food, including honey and fish. Some foods are entirely poisonous or have components that are poisonous if not properly prepared (crab and some fish are among the most common culprits).

When faced with suspected food poisoning, ask what food has been eaten in the last 48 hours. Food poisoning can take some time to show (however, toxic food poisoning tends to act much more quickly). Be alert to the possibility of food poisoning if there is any combination of the following:

SIGNS AND SYMPTOMS

- Nausea and vomiting
- Stomach cramps
- Diarrhea
- Fever
- Aches and pains
- Signs of shock (see pages 44–45)

Symptons of toxic poisoning are dizziness, slurred speech, and difficulty breathing and swallowing.

- Strange-tasting food or food that has been left out in the heat.
- Several people with the same symptoms.
- Undercooked or reheated food.

TREATMENT

1 Monitor and maintain the person's airway and breathing (see pages 12–17). If there are breathing difficulties, call 911.

2 Help the person into a comfortable position.

3 Call for medical advice on treatment and care.

4 Give plenty of fluids to drink, particularly if the person has vomiting and diarrhea.

5 Support the person if he or she vomits, providing a bowl and towel as necessary.

Do not underestimate food poisoning, particularly in the very young or the elderly.

COMMON POISONOUS PLANTS

Many plants have components that are mildly poisonous if eaten, or that may cause a reaction if they are touched.

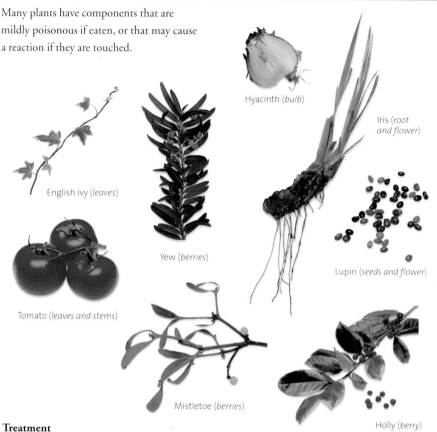

Hyacinth (*bulb*)

Iris (*root and flower*)

English ivy (*leaves*)

Yew (*berries*)

Lupin (*seeds and flower*)

Tomato (*leaves and stems*)

Mistletoe (*berries*)

Holly (*berry*)

Treatment

If you suspect that somebody has eaten a poisonous plant, attempt to identify it and seek medical advice. If the person is having breathing difficulties or appears to be lapsing into unconsciousness, call 911. Be prepared to resuscitate (see pages 29–33) if necessary.

Some other common poisonous plants

Daffodil (*bulbs*)
Deadly nightshade (*roots and berries*)
Mushrooms (*many wild mushrooms and toadstools*)
Rhubarb leaves

Miscarriage

A miscarriage is the loss of a pregnancy in the first 24 weeks. There are many causes of miscarriage, and for some parents the reason for their loss will never be known. About a fifth of all pregnancies end in miscarriage, most of these before the twelfth week.

TREATMENT

1 Overall, listen to the wants and needs of the woman. She will often be very distressed and scared. When possible, help her to a position of privacy and if possible, ensure that she is treated by another woman and has support from her partner or friend.

2 If bleeding or pain is severe, or there are signs of shock, call 911.

Listen to the woman and give reassurance and support

Above

A woman who has had a miscarriage needs to be treated sensitively. Reassure her and monitor for signs of shock while waiting for an ambulance to arrive.

SUPPORT GROUPS

Most women who have a miscarriage do not have problems with subsequent pregnancies but a woman should take time to grieve and talk about her feelings before becoming pregnant again. Group therapy with others who have had the same experience is a good way of helping a woman come to terms with the loss of her baby. The woman's doctor should be able to provide details of appropriate support groups in her area.

3 Reassure the woman and offer her a sanitary pad or towel.

4 Keep anything that is passed from the vagina out of sight of the woman, for medical staff to examine.

SIGNS AND SYMPTOMS

- Bleeding—this may be light spotting over a number of days and/or a sudden heavy bloodflow
- Period-like pain or pain in the lower back
- Potential signs and symptoms of shock, caused by blood loss (see pages 44–45)
- Passing the fetus and other products associated with birth (this may just look like a heavy blood clot)

Many miscarriages can take several days from start to finish and may not start with a heavy bloodflow or severe pain. Some women who are miscarrying may not have realized that they were pregnant because many miscarriages take place in the first weeks after conception.

Pregnant women suffering unusual bleeding should always seek early medical advice from their doctor or midwife. An investigation may show that the pregnancy has not ended or that miscarriage is threatened but not inevitable.

OTHER EMERGENCY PROBLEMS WITH PREGNANCY

Ectopic pregnancy

In this circumstance, the fertilized egg has become embedded in the Fallopian tube rather than the womb. As well as ending the pregnancy, this is a potentially life-threatening condition for the mother. The woman will usually have severe pain in the abdominal area, with potential bleeding and signs of shock. Call 911 immediately.

Embryo develops in Fallopian tube instead of uterus

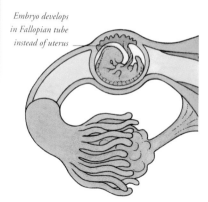

Placenta previa/placental abruption

Bleeding in later pregnancy is more unusual. A painless bright red bloodflow may indicate that something is seriously wrong with the placenta, causing potential life-threatening problems for both the mother and child. Support the mother in a position of rest, call 911 and treat for shock (see pages 44–45).

Emergency Childbirth

It is very unlikely that you will have to deliver a child in an unplanned-for situation. Even the second stage of labor can allow enough time for an ambulance or midwife to arrive. However, if you are called upon to help with an emergency birth, take comfort from the fact that there is little that you can do to affect the birth process. Your key role is to support the mother, to ensure that medical help has been called, and to care for the mother and baby after the birth.

WHAT CAN YOU DO TO HELP?

1 Ensure that the midwife or doctor has been called. If labor is in the early stages, ask the mother where she wants to be and make arrangements for transport.

2 If at any time there is severe bleeding or signs and symptoms of shock (see pages 44–45), call 911.

**SIGNS THAT THE BIRTH
MAY BE IMMINENT**

- Contractions less than 2 minutes apart
- Strong urge to push
- Bulging vaginal opening
- Baby's head visible

If the urge to bear down comes on the way to hospital, the mother can try using breathing techniques to avoid pushing.

---

3 Support the mother in her most comfortable position. This will usually be standing or squatting—gravity helps the delivery process. Ask her what she would like you to do to help with the pain. Potential options include a warm bath, rubbing the small of her back, and offering frequent sips of water. Encourage her to breathe out as breath-holding makes pain worse by increasing muscle tension. Most pregnant women will have a pregnancy record. Help her to find this because it contains useful information for both you and the medical staff.

4 If labor has progressed to the second stage and birth is imminent, ensure that:

- The woman has removed the clothes from her lower body.
- The ambulance is on the way—the ambulance control or midwife may give you instructions over the phone.
- You and the environment are as clean as they can be.
- You have a warm covering for the baby and mother.

5 Help the mother into a position she finds comfortable.

6 Support the mother while she pushes out the baby as it descends.

7 Support the head and shoulders as the baby appears—this will happen naturally and quickly. Do not pull the baby. If the cord is wrapped around the neck, check that it is loose and gently pull it over the head.

Supporting woman on a birthing stool

Mother stays vertical throughout

Above
Positions such as squatting, kneeling, sitting, or standing can all help to relieve pain. A birthing stool allows the mother to remain vertical and use gravity to help push the baby out.

IF THE BABY IS BREECH (NOT HEAD FIRST)

The concern with a breech birth is that the largest part of the baby (the head) may not be easily delivered. If the baby is breech a foot, knee, or buttock may come out first. If this happens:

1 Ensure that medical help has been called.

2 Allow the birth to continue—do not try to stop the baby coming out.

3 Support the baby's body as it is delivered.

4 If the head is not delivered within 3 minutes of the shoulders, gently raise the baby's legs to the ceiling until you can see the face (do not pull the baby from the mother). Wipe the face clear and encourage the mother to keep pushing until the head is delivered.

8 Gently lift the baby and place on the mother's stomach. There is no need to cut the cord. If the baby does not show any signs of movement, check its airway and breathing (see pages 12–17) and be prepared to resuscitate (see pages 29–33) if necessary.

9 Keep mother and baby warm while waiting for the ambulance. The placenta and cord will follow shortly—keep these for the medical staff to check. Gently massaging below the navel may help stop bleeding.

Everyday First Aid

Nosebleeds

Nosebleeds are very common among children and many start spontaneously. Unless they are a direct result of an impact to the nose, the cause may not be known. Simple treatment whereby the blood is encouraged to clot is usually effective. The priority is to protect the victim's airway and to try and prevent blood from being swallowed (see also pages 87–91).

HOW TO TREAT NOSEBLEEDS

1 Lean the child forward and encourage her to spit blood into a handkerchief or some other receptacle.

2 Pinch the child's nose just below the hard part at its top and apply firm pressure for 10 minutes (this is the amount of time it takes for a clot to form). If the bleeding has not stopped after 10 minutes, apply pressure for two further periods of 10 minutes. If bleeding continues then take the child to hospital.

Once the bleeding has stopped, advise the child not to scratch, pick, or blow her nose, not to drink hot liquid, and not to exert herself, because all these activities can dislodge the clot and cause the bleeding to start again.

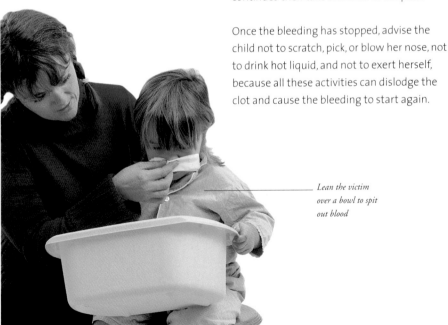

Lean the victim over a bowl to spit out blood

Minor Wounds

Most minor wounds can be treated in the home without the need for further medical attention.
First aid treatment can promote recovery and prevent infection. However, further medical
advice should be sought if: there is a foreign body embedded in the wound; the wound shows
signs of infection; the wound has the potential for tetanus and the injured person's
immunization is not up-to-date; the wound is from a human or animal bite.

TREATING MINOR WOUNDS If possible, wash your hands before treating the wound. Check that there is nothing in the wound. If the wound is dirty, clean it under running water. Pat dry with clean, non-fluffy material. Clean the wound from the center out with gauze swabs or antiseptic wipes, using a fresh piece for each wipe. Cover the wound with an adhesive dressing to apply pressure and protect from infection. Elevate the wound if necessary to help control bleeding.

1 Check there is nothing embedded in the wound and clean and dry it.

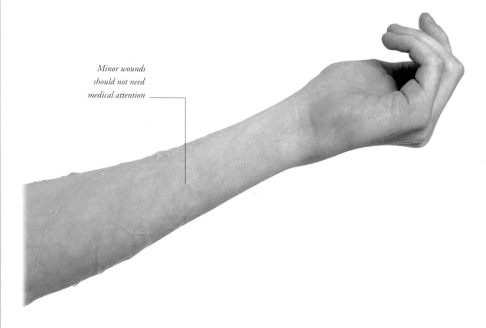

Minor wounds should not need medical attention

2 Clean the wound with antiseptic wipes or swabs, then cover it with a dressing for protection and to apply pressure.

3 Raise the wound if necessary to reduce blood flow to the affected area.

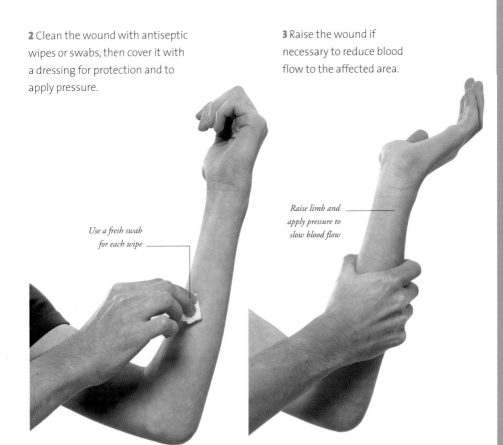

Use a fresh swab for each wipe

Raise limb and apply pressure to slow blood flow

IF THERE IS GRAVEL OR GRIT IN THE WOUND

If there is loose debris on the wound this can be easily washed away with water or taken off by gently dabbing with clean gauze. If there are small bits of debris embedded into the wound these should be treated as foreign bodies. Gently cover with a clean dressing and bandage the dressing into place, taking care not to press on the embedded debris. Raise the injured part if appropriate and seek medical advice.

BRUISING A bruise is the sign of internal bleeding. Usually caused by direct impact, bruises are sometimes painful but generally heal swiftly with little intervention needed.

A bruise goes through several changes in appearance as it heals and may not appear for some time, even days, after the accident. Initially, the injured part may be red from the impact; over time this may become blue as blood seeps into the injured tissue; as it heals it becomes brown and then fades to yellow.

Severe bruising can also be the sign of serious internal bleeding. If bruising is extensive and is accompanied by any of the following signs and symptoms, assume that serious internal bleeding is present. Treat the injured person for shock and seek medical help.

SIGNS AND SYMPTOMS OF INTERNAL BLEEDING

- Victim is known to have had an accident (not necessarily in the immediate past)
- Signs and symptoms of shock
- Bruising
- Boarding—this most commonly occurs where there is bleeding into the stomach area; the quantity of blood combined with the tissues swelling results in a rigidity to the tissues
- Swelling
- Bleeding from body orifices (see Bleeding from Special Sites, pages 87–89)

Most bruises, however, are not serious. First aid can reduce pain and promote recovery from an uncomfortable bruise.

Soak a towel in cold water then wring out

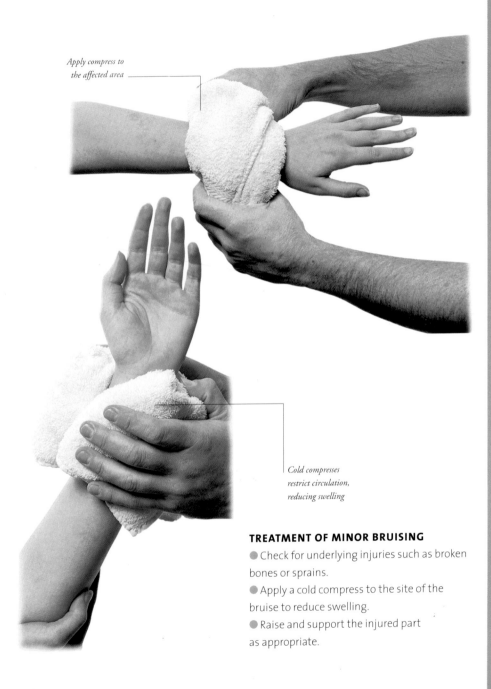

Apply compress to the affected area

Cold compresses restrict circulation, reducing swelling

TREATMENT OF MINOR BRUISING

- Check for underlying injuries such as broken bones or sprains.
- Apply a cold compress to the site of the bruise to reduce swelling.
- Raise and support the injured part as appropriate.

Infected Wounds

Any injury that pierces the skin can become infected. Infection is caused by germs entering the body, either through the object causing the injury (for example, a dirty knife) or from sources after the injury occurred. Cuts, burns, bites, stings, and open fractures all carry with them a risk of infection.

PREVENTING INFECTION There are a number of things that you can do to reduce the risk of infection.

● When time permits (for example, for non-life-threatening, less serious injuries), wash your hands thoroughly before treating an open wound.
● Wear gloves if available.

● Try to reduce direct contact with the open wound—for example, ask the injured person to apply pressure with her own hand if possible.
● Cover injuries as soon as practicable.
● Do not cough over injuries—turn away and cover your mouth.
● Advise the injured person to check that her tetanus immunization is up-to-date.

Above
Wash your hands thoroughly under running water before treating an open wound if you have time to do so. This will reduce the risk of transmitting germs into the wound.

Above
A disposable rubber glove is an ideal barrier method to prevent contamination of a wound. Keep a pair in the top of your first aid kit to reduce direct contact with the wound.

Above
Ask the person who has been injured to apply pressure with her own hand if possible to reduce direct contact with an open wound and lessen the risk of infection.

SIGNS AND SYMPTOMS OF INFECTION

If the following signs and symptoms develop after an open wound is inflicted, the injured person should seek immediate medical attention:

- Increased pain
- Swelling
- Redness around the site of the wound
- Discharge from the site
- Unpleasant smell from the site of the wound
- Red tracks from the site to the heart
- Swollen glands
- Failure to heal

TREATING AN INFECTED WOUND

1 Cover the wound with a sterile dressing and bandage into place.

2 Raise the injured part if possible, to reduce swelling and pain.

3 Seek early medical advice. Treat for shock if necessary (see pages 44–45).

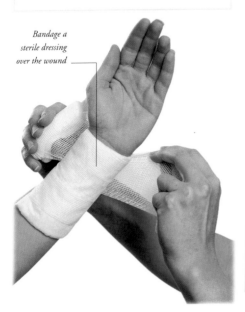

Bandage a sterile dressing over the wound

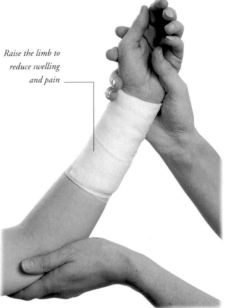

Raise the limb to reduce swelling and pain

Dealing with Splinters and Fish Hooks

Large objects embedded in a wound, or foreign objects near to a vulnerable site such as the eye, need special care and medical treatment. Smaller debris, such as shards of glass or splinters of wood, stuck into minor wounds can usually be successfully managed at home without further treatment.

REMOVING SPLINTERS

1 If the splinter is fully embedded in the skin, clean the wound, cover gently, and seek medical attention. If part of the splinter is out of the skin, you may try to remove it with tweezers.

2 Pass the tweezers over a flame to clean them and reduce the risk of infection.

3 Use the tweezers to grasp the end of the object and to gently pull it out at the same angle that it went in. If the splinter breaks off in the wound or is not easy to remove, treat it as you would a larger foreign body (see pages 170–173).

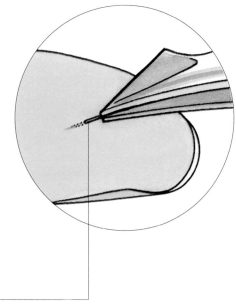

Use tweezers to grip and remove a splinter

4 Once removed, squeeze the wound to express a small amount of blood, clean the site with soap and water, and gently cover with a plaster or dressing as appropriate.

5 Splinters can carry infection into the body so check the site for any signs of infection over the coming days. Tetanus is a particular risk, especially if the splinter was obtained while gardening, so check the date of the person's last tetanus immunization and seek a booster if necessary.

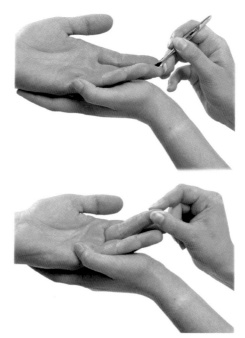

FISH HOOKS While the injuries associated with an embedded fish hook may be relatively minor, they are particularly difficult to remove because of their barbed ends. Only try to remove one if medical help is not readily available, for example, if you are on a boat.

WHEN MEDICAL HELP IS EASY TO ACCESS
1 Cut the line as close to the hook as possible to prevent it catching on something and causing further damage.

2 Pad around the hook until you can bandage over or around it without pushing it further in.

3 Seek medical help to ensure there is no underlying damage to the tissues.

WHEN MEDICAL HELP MAY TAKE SOME TIME TO ARRIVE

If you can see the barb:

1 Cut the line as close to the hook as possible.

2 Cut the barb away and carefully remove the hook by its eye.

3 Clean and cover the wound and elevate if it is on a limb.

4 Check the wound for signs of infection over the coming days and check that the person's tetanus booster is up-to-date.

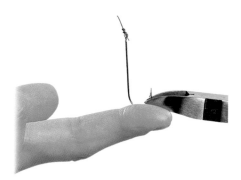

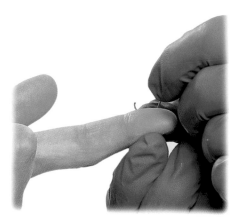

TREATING A LARGER EMBEDDED OBJECT

- Do not attempt to remove the object.
- Apply pressure to the wound by padding around the base of the object over the top of sterile gauze or a piece of clean material.
- Bandage over the padding to apply pressure without moving the object.
- If the object is embedded in an arm or leg, elevation may help to reduce bleeding and pain.
- Seek medical help.

If the object is very long, provide additional support at its base to prevent it from moving.

If you cannot see the barb:

1 If you are able, push the hook quickly and firmly forward through the skin until the barb can be seen.

2 Cut the barb away and then treat as outlined above.

If the barb cannot be easily removed, do not attempt to remove the hook—instead, treat as for a larger embedded object (see box).

Foreign Bodies

Children are prone to putting objects into their nose, ears, and mouth. If left for some time, such objects can cause infection that may result in permanent damage. Young children are also liable to swallow small objects. These usually pass through the system and can be identified in the bowel movement as having safely moved through the body. Larger or sharp objects pose a greater risk of internal injury. If there are signs of difficulty breathing, the object may have gone down the windpipe rather than the tube to the stomach (esophagus). Call 911 and follow the procedures for choking on pages 36-37. (For general procedures, see pages 34–39.)

FOREIGN BODIES IN THE EAR
Treatment
Do not attempt to remove an object from the ear—you are likely to push it in further, causing more damage, particularly to the eardrum. Reassure the child and take her to hospital.

SIGNS AND SYMPTOMS OF A FOREIGN BODY IN THE EAR

- Pain
- Temporary deafness
- Discharge

SIGNS AND SYMPTOMS OF AN INSECT IN THE EAR

- Very loud buzzing/ringing noise in the ear
- Pain or discomfort

INSECT IN THE EAR
Treatment
1 Sit the child down and reassure him before giving treatment.

2 Lean the child's head toward the unaffected side and pour tepid water into the ear with the aim of floating the insect out.

3 If this does not work, take the child to hospital as soon as possible.

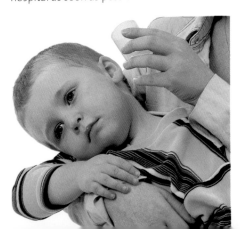

FOREIGN BODIES IN THE NOSE The key priority with any object in the nose is the maintenance of a clear airway. If at any time the object appears to be making breathing difficult, follow the procedures for choking (see pages 34–39) and make a call for emergency assistance.

Treatment

1 Sit the child down, and reassure him.

2 Encourage the child to breathe through his mouth rather than his nose.

3 Do not attempt to remove the object as you may push it further in, causing more damage.

4 Take the child to the hospital so that the object can be removed.

SIGNS AND SYMPTOMS OF A FOREIGN BODY IN THE NOSE

- Pain
- Swelling
- Discharge (if the object has been there for some time)
- Breathing difficulties
- A snoring sound on breathing

FOREIGN BODIES IN THE EYE Small items stuck to the white of the eye can be very irritating but are usually easy to remove. If an item is embedded in the eye or is stuck on the colored part of the eye (the iris), do not attempt to remove it. Cover the eye as appropriate and take the person to hospital for treatment.

Treatment

1 Sit the person down facing the light so that you can clearly see what needs to be removed.

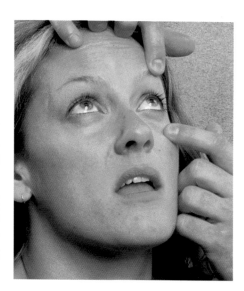

2 Examine the eye by gently separating the eyelids with your finger and thumb. Ask the person to move the eye up and down and from left to right. Allow the person to blink.

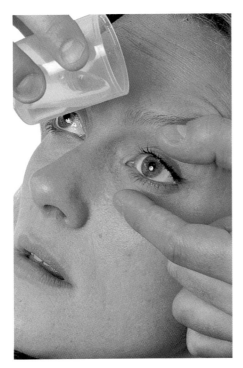

SWALLOWED OBJECTS
Treatment

If the object was very large, sharp, or potentially poisonous (for example, some kinds of battery), call 911. If the object was small and smooth, take the child to a doctor or hospital as soon as possible.

3 If you can see the foreign body and it is not embedded or touching the colored part of the eye, gently wash it out. Tilt the head to one side and run water through the eye, holding the eyelid open. Continue with this treatment for up to 30 minutes, allowing the person to blink regularly.

4 If washing does not work and the object is not embedded in the eye, try to remove it with a moist piece of clean cloth.

5 If you remain unable to remove the object, take the person to hospital.

INHALED OBJECTS It is possible for small and smooth objects to be inhaled into the lungs. This may cause difficulty breathing, particularly if the objects are porous and swell up on contact with body fluids. Small nuts are a particular risk, with the added concern that some people have a severe allergic reaction to them.

Below

Carefully check the mouth for any object that can be reached with a finger.

SIGNS AND SYMPTOMS OF AN INHALED OBJECT

● Choking noises which pass as the object moves into the lung
● Hacking cough
● Difficulty breathing
● Ask bystanders what happened and look around for evidence of bags of nuts, sweets, etc.

Below

You may need to perform the Heimlich Maneuver to remove the obstruction.

Treatment

1 If the person is unable to take a breath, treat her for choking if necessary (see pages 34–37), and perform the Heimlich Maneuver to displace the obstruction.

2 Call 911 as soon as possible and monitor breathing while waiting.

3 Reassure the person and try to find out exactly what was inhaled.

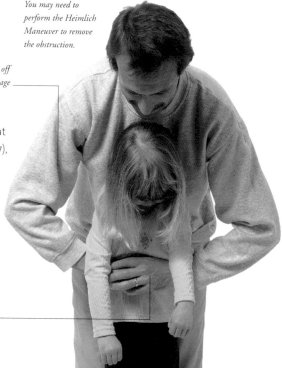

Keep your arms off the child's rib cage

Give 4 short thrusts inward and upward

Animal Bites

There is a risk of infection with any animal bite, no matter how small. The bite should be assessed by a doctor as soon as possible to see if a tetanus or rabies injection, or a course of antibiotics, is required. First aid treatment for bites is to keep the wound clean and control any bleeding.

ANIMAL BITES Any animal bite requires medical attention. Deep bites can cause serious wounds, severe bleeding, and tissue damage, while all animal bites can cause infection. Puncture wounds from teeth carry infection deep into the tissue, while scratches are also an infection risk. The human bite is among the most infectious.

CHECKING FOR INFECTION

Warn the injured person to watch for signs of an infected wound over the coming days. Seek immediate medical attention if any combination of the following signs and symptoms develops:

- Increased pain
- Swelling
- Redness around the site of the wound
- Discharge from the site
- Unpleasant smell from the site of the wound
- Red tracks from the site of the wound to the heart
- Swollen glands

TREATMENT

The priority is to ensure the safety of yourself and bystanders. If the animal is still a risk, do not approach it but call the local Animal Control Service through your police department.

For serious wounds

1 Help the injured person sit down to help reduce shock (see pages 44–45).

2 Treat any bleeding by:
- Looking in the wound
- Applying direct pressure
- Elevating the site if it is a limb

3 Take or send the person to hospital.

For smaller wounds and scratches

1 Wash the wound thoroughly with soap and water.

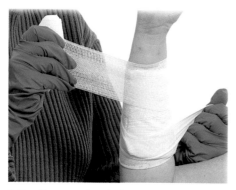

2 Dry the wound with clean gauze or other non-fluffy material and cover with a dressing.

3 Seek medical advice.

SPECIFIC INFECTIONS SPREAD BY BITES

Rabies

Rabies is an increasingly rare but potentially very serious, even fatal, condition carried by animal bites. Rabies in the US is rare, but if the bite is from an animal that may have come into the country without going through normal checks, or if you are bitten overseas, then seek immediate medical attention. There is no cure for rabies but early vaccination following a bite can help develop immunity.

Hepatitis B and C

There is a small chance that hepatitis B and C may be transmitted by a human bite. If concerned, seek medical advice.

Tetanus

Tetanus bacteria carry a particular risk when carried deep into a wound with jagged edges or a puncture wound. Animal bites carry a potential risk of tetanus. Tetanus affects the central nervous system and can cause muscle spasms, breathing problems, and sometimes death. It is also known as lockjaw because it may tense up the jaw muscles. There is a vaccination for tetanus but immunity is not lifelong and anybody suffering a potentially hazardous injury should seek medical advice on having a booster injection.

Insect Bites and Stings

Insect bites and stings are painful and there are many insects native to the US that carry potentially fatal venom. Dangerous biting insects include spiders such as the black widow, brown recluse, and some tarantulas; stinging insects include scorpions, wasps, and bees. Children and the elderly are most at risk but even so, stings and insect bites rarely kill unless there is an allergic reaction. Stings in the mouth or throat are also dangerous because the swelling they cause can block the airway. In all cases, avoidance is the best defense.

STINGS AND BITES A sting is felt as a sudden sharp pain and appears as a raised white patch on a reddened area of skin. A bite is less painful and usually causes mild discomfort and skin inflammation.

POTENTIALLY LIFE-THREATENING RESPONSES TO STINGS AND BITES
Anaphylaxis
This is an allergic reaction to a substance with which the body is in contact (see pages 50–52). Bee stings are among the most common cause. Anaphylaxis can develop within seconds and can be fatal.

Multiple stings
While one sting is unlikely to cause problems on a major scale for an otherwise healthy adult, several stings may provoke a dangerous response.

Effects of venom
Some venoms kill the cells around the bite or sting mark, are slow to heal, and leave deep scars. In rare cases, they can be fatal. Other venoms affect the nervous system and require an anti-venom medicine or they may be fatal.

STINGS TO MOUTH AND THROAT Any sting to the mouth or throat should be treated with care because subsequent swelling may cause difficulty with breathing.

SIGNS AND SYMPTOMS OF A LIFE-THREATENING REACTION

- Difficulty breathing
- Swollen lips, tongue, and throat
- Blotchy skin
- Victim has felt a bite or sting (sometimes this may be described as a scratch)
- Pain, swelling, and reddening over the site of the bite or sting

Treatment

1 Monitor and maintain airway and breathing (see pages 12–17). Be prepared to resuscitate (see pages 29–33) if necessary.

2 If the victim is a known sufferer of anaphylaxis, he may have an auto-injector that contains life-saving medicine. Help him to find this as quickly as possible and, if necessary, help to administer it.

3 If the victim is conscious, help into the most comfortable position (this will usually be sitting up).

4 If the sting was in the mouth, give the victim an ice cube to suck or frequent sips of cold water.

5 Call 911 and explain what has happened, identifying the insect if possible.

6 Make an attempt to identify what the victim has been bitten or stung by but do not put yourself at risk.

ORDINARY BITES AND STINGS
Treatment

1 If you can see the sting, remove it by flicking with the edge of a piece of plastic such as a credit card, or with tweezers. Take care not to squeeze the poison sac at the end of the sting.

2 Wash the affected area to reduce the risk of infection entering the wound.

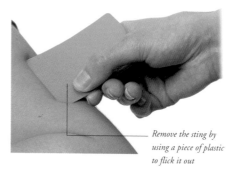

Remove the sting by using a piece of plastic to flick it out

Use a cold compress to reduce swelling

3 Apply a cold compress to the site to reduce pain and swelling.

4 Remove rings, watches, or anything likely to cause a constriction if the area swells.

5 Advise the victim to see a doctor if pain persists or there are any signs of infection.

SIGNS AND SYMPTOMS

- Reddening, pain, and swelling over the site of the sting
- Person has felt a bite or sting
- Sting left in the skin (if from a bee)

More on Bites and Stings

The general guidance for dealing with bites and stings is: to monitor airway and breathing (see pages 12–17); be prepared to resuscitate (see pages 29–33) if necessary; to support and reassure the injured person; to offer relief with a cold compress; and to avoid infection by cleaning and covering the wound. In addition, there are some specific treatments that may be useful for certain types of bites and stings.

TICKS

Ticks are tiny bloodsucking creatures found in long grass that attach themselves to animals and humans firmly by embedding their mouthparts into the skin. Ticks cause discomfort and can transmit disease. Although simple to remove, great care should be taken because the mouthparts could remain in the skin if removed incorrectly. Use a flat-ended pair of tweezers or gloved fingers and grasp the tick at its head end, as close to the skin as possible. Using even pressure, pull the tick straight up, avoiding twisting and squeezing the tick's body. Once it has been removed, clean and cover the bitten area.

MOSQUITOES

Mosquitoes are small airborne insects. They feed on animals, including humans, by injecting a minute amount of anesthetic and a chemical that stops blood from clotting and then sucking blood from their host until they are full. Unfortunately this can leave a small inflamed area that is uncomfortable but not life-threatening. This can be easily treated by a cold compress.

In many countries mosquitoes carry malaria, which can be fatal. Should you visit countries that have malarial areas, you must seek advice from your doctor on how to protect yourself and which antimalarial drugs are best suited to you.

JELLYFISH

There are a few species of jellyfish that are poisonous. Generally those that are poisonous have long tentacles that sway freely beneath their bodies and contain stingers that inject chemicals into anyone that should come too close. Although not normally fatal, they can cause extreme pain that leads to panic, especially in children, which can lead to further danger in the water. A sting may also cause anaphylactic shock in some people.

These stings can be treated by calming the victim and then applying alcohol or vinegar to the affected area for a minimum of 3 minutes or until the pain subsides.

Should the victim suffer a severe allergic reaction (see pages 50–52), emergency medical aid should be sought.

Pour vinegar onto a jellyfish sting to reduce pain

TOADFISH

There are many marine creatures that can cause pain and infection if you step on them. Toadfish are found off the US Atlantic and Gulf coasts. They are small fish that bury themselves in the sand, usually in shallows where they hunt. They have sharp spines on their dorsal fin that can inject poison into anyone who steps on them.

Although the pain is extreme, it can be quickly relieved by placing the affected area in a bowl of water as hot as the sufferer can stand for 20 minutes or until the pain subsides. Make sure you test the hot water with your elbow first because otherwise you may scald the skin.

If the victim suffers a severe reaction, emergency medical aid should be sought.

Headaches

Headaches have many causes. Often they can develop for no apparent reason or as a symptom of common illnesses such as flu. Sometimes they are an indicator of a more serious condition such as a head injury, stroke, or other serious illness.

TREATMENT

1 Settle the person into a comfortable position in a quiet place. Consider remedies such as dimming the lights, applying a cold compress, providing fresh air, and encouraging sips of cold water.

2 Check for other signs and symptoms that may indicate a more serious condition and take action as appropriate. Seek urgent medical advice if:

- There has been a head injury.
- There are signs and symptoms of meningitis.
- The person appears confused, drowsy, or there is any fall in the level of consciousness (see pages 61–63).

3 Help the person to take her usual painkillers.

4 If the pain persists, seek medical advice.

SYMPTOMS OF TENSION HEADACHES

- Sensation of a band tightening around the skull
- Pain ranges in intensity
- A throbbing sensation that pulses in time with the heartbeat
- May be accompanied by eye or neck pain

SIGNS AND SYMPTOMS OF MENINGITIS

Any combination of the following may be present:

- Fever
- Headache
- Nausea or vomiting
- Stiff neck (pain or difficulty in touching the chest with the chin)
- Convulsions
- Sensitivity to light
- Rash (bleeding under the skin) which does not go away if a glass is pressed against it

In addition, in babies and young children:
- The soft spot on the head (the fontanelle) may be stretched tight
- There may be floppiness, lack of focus on surroundings

Fever

A person's normal temperature is between 96.8–100.4°F. A fever occurs when the temperature remains higher than this for some time. Most fevers are caused by infection, either infection associated with diseases such as flu, meningitis, or chickenpox, or with a local infection, such as may follow a bite or an open wound. Most fevers pass with minimal risk but a temperature over 104°F can indicate a serious infection and medical advice should be sought. High temperatures, particularly in young children, can cause febrile convulsions (see page 60).

TAKING A TEMPERATURE

A raised temperature is a sign that the body is fighting off an infection. There are several types of thermometer that can measure the body's temperature. One of the most accurate is a mercury thermometer, in which a narrow column of mercury expands in response to heat and moves up to a point on a clearly marked scale. Take a temperature on the forehead, in the mouth, under the arm or, if you have an appropriate thermometer, in the ear. Do not take a child's mouth temperature if you are using a mercury thermometer—she may bite it and swallow mercury, which is a poison.

Strip thermometers are easy to use to take a temperature

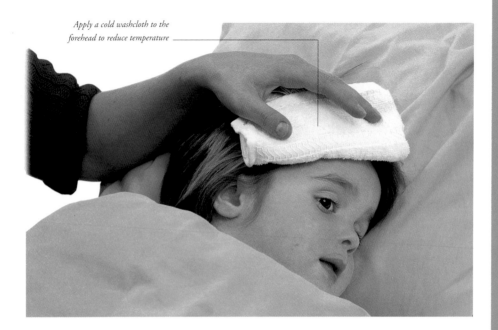

Apply a cold washcloth to the forehead to reduce temperature

TREATMENT

1 Make the person comfortable. Ensure that the surrounding air is cool (open a window or use a fan) and provide cool washcloths or sponges. Take care not to overcool.

2 Give the person plenty of cool drinks. Encourage the person to sip these slowly to prevent feeling nauseous.

3 Look for any other signs of infection, such as rashes or swollen glands, and seek medical advice if you are unsure of the cause or seriousness of the condition.

4 Enable the person to take her usual analgesics. Acetaminophen acts as an antipyretic, which means that it will help reduce a fever as well as bring pain relief. Non-steroidal anti-inflammatories (NSAIDS) such as ibuprofen are good for bringing down fever. Children should take medicine appropriate for their age.

SIGNS AND SYMPTOMS OF FEVER

- Raised temperature
- Pale skin (becoming red as the temperature rises)
- Feeling shaky and shivery
- Increasing aches, pain, and headache as the temperature rises

Earache, Toothache, and Sore Throat

Earache can be exceptionally painful. It has a number of common causes, including infection, or as a symptom of other conditions such as flu or tonsillitis. Like earache, toothache can cause agonizing pain. Usually caused by a decaying or damaged tooth, it can also arise as a result of problems such as an ear infection or sinusitis, or even from jaw tension. In babies and children, there may be pain and discomfort as their teeth come through. Sore throats can be a sign of infection such as tonsillitis or a symptom of colds and flu. There may be swelling and infection around the throat, or swollen glands visible under the jaw.

TREATING EARACHE

1 If there is a fever or discharge, seek urgent medical help, as this may be a sign of serious infection or a burst eardrum. Seek medical advice if there is any loss of hearing. Check the history of the problem to rule out injury to the ear or skull, or the presence of a foreign object.

2 Assist the person into a comfortable position. A hot-water bottle wrapped in a towel placed on the ear may provide some pain relief.

3 Enable the person to take her usual analgesics.

4 If the condition persists or gets worse, especially in children, seek medical advice.

Hold a hot-water bottle against the ear to relieve pain

ANALGESICS (PAINKILLERS)

When used according to the instructions, analgesics such as acetaminophen have little risk for a healthy adult. Medicines such as acetaminophen syrup made especially for children can provide safe pain relief.

People in severe pain are at risk from an accidental overdose of analgesics and while paracetamol is generally safe, one of its potential drawbacks is that very few extra pills are required to risk an overdose.

To reduce the chances of problems with any analgesics:

● Read and follow the instructions carefully.
● Seek advice from your doctor or pharmacist if necessary.
● Do not leave analgesics near the bed while sleeping. It is easy to wake up in pain and forget when the last dose was taken.
● Seek early medical advice if you think that an overdose may have been taken, even if there are no signs and symptoms of a problem. Acetaminophen poisoning, for example, does not show up immediately but the antidote needs to be taken as soon as possible.

TREATING A SORE THROAT

1 Check the history of the problem to rule out poisoning or burns.

2 Give the person plenty of cold fluids to drink.

3 Enable the person to take his usual analgesics.

4 Seek medical advice if the condition persists or if sore throats are recurrent, particularly in children.

TREATING TOOTHACHE

1 Check the history of the problem to rule out any injury to the mouth or jaw.

2 Assist the person into a comfortable position. The throbbing pain associated with an infected tooth is often eased if the person is sitting up.

3 Enable the person to take her usual analgesics.

4 A hot-water bottle wrapped in a towel or hot compress placed alongside the face may help relieve the pain. Oil of cloves applied to a cotton swab and placed on the tooth (not the gums) may also help numb the pain. Children may benefit from teething remedies available from pharmacies.

5 Encourage the person to make an appointment with a dentist.

Dab the tooth with oil of cloves to reduce pain

Abdominal Pain

Pain in the abdomen can range from mild discomfort to agony. There are many causes of abdominal pain. Most are not serious but others may be an indication of serious injury, such as internal bleeding, of a potential medical emergency such as appendicitis or a stomach ulcer, or of problems with the muscles, for example, a hernia or muscle strain. If stomach pain in an infant is accompanied by fever, diarrhea, or vomiting, seek prompt medical advice.

Type of pain	Other symptoms	Possible causes
Generalized stomachache	Nausea, tearfulness, clinginess	Stress
Generalized stomachache	Sore throat, fever, blocked nose	Throat infection, cold
Sudden pain causing baby to scream and draw up legs	Baby under four months of age	Colic
Severe pain near navel that moves right	Temperature, lack of appetite, vomiting	Appendicitis

TREATING ABDOMINAL PAIN

1 Check the history of the pain to rule out recent injury, potential poisoning (see pages 141–143), or an underlying medical condition.

2 Settle the person into a comfortable position and provide a covered hot-water bottle to provide some relief from the pain.

3 If the pain is severe or does not ease within half an hour, seek medical advice.

Seek early medical advice or an ambulance if the pain is accompanied by:

● Vomiting red blood (a potential burst stomach ulcer).
● High temperature (possible infection, such as peritonitis, caused by a burst appendix).
● Rigid (inflexible) abdomen (may indicate internal bleeding).
● Signs of shock (see pages 44–45).

Vomiting and Diarrhea

Severe vomiting and diarrhoea can be very serious, particularly in children and the elderly, who are more vulnerable to the accompanying risk of dehydration. The loss of circulating body fluid can lead to life-threatening shock (see pages 44–45) if it is not replaced.

CAUSES Likely causes of vomiting and diarrhea include: food poisoning; viral infections such as gastroenteritis; and sensitivity to a new or unusual food. Vomiting alone can also accompany some medical conditions such as concussion and compression (see Skull Fractures, pages 96–97) and other injuries.

TREATMENT

1 Check the person's recent history for clues as to the cause and to rule out underlying injury such as a serious blow to the head.

2 Help the person into a comfortable position. If he is vomiting, this will usually be sitting up. Help the person to the bathroom as necessary.

3 Help the person to clean himself up and to change clothes as necessary.

4 Provide bland fluids (except milk) to drink slowly—it is important to keep fluid levels up.

5 Seek medical advice if the condition persists. If the person shows signs of shock, seek urgent medical attention.

ISOTONIC DRINKS

These drinks replace vital fluids and important minerals and sugars in the body. Available to purchase ready made, you can also make your own.

Add
1 tsp salt and
5 tsp sugar
per 2 pints of water or diluted orange juice

This drink should be taken in short sips as needed.

Cramps

Cramps are muscle spasms generally caused by exercising and loss of fluid, for example, through heatstroke (see pages 139–140). However, they can also occur spontaneously, often at night, particularly in older people. Common sites for cramps include the sole of the foot, the calf, and the thigh. If the abdominal muscles are affected, the condition is known as a stitch.

TREATING CRAMPS A gentle stretching and massage of the affected area will help to relieve cramps. Give the affected person plenty of fluids and something salty to eat.

FOR THE THIGH

1 Straighten the knee and raise the leg if the cramp is in the back of the leg.

2 Bend the knee if the cramp is in the front of the thigh.

3 Massage the affected muscle firmly.

Straighten leg and massage affected muscle firmly

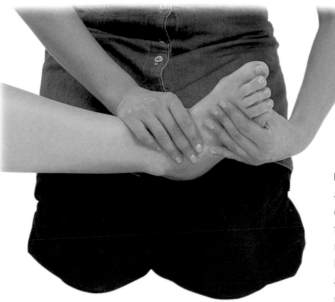

FOR A FOOT Often if the affected person stands on the foot with the sole flat on the ground, this may relieve the pain. If this does not work, accompany this with gentle massage.

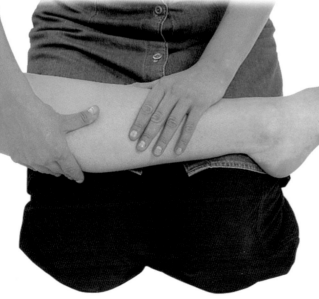

FOR THE CALF Straighten the person's knee and gently push the foot up toward the shin. Massage the affected muscle.

Hysteria, Panic Attacks, and Hiccups

The word hysteria has come to mean the extreme behavior exhibited at time of high emotion. This can be positive emotion, for example, delight at a pop concert, or negative emotion, for example, the shock of hearing bad news. Hiccups are caused by an involuntary contraction of the diaphragm, the muscle that separates the lung and stomach cavities. They are very common and although not serious can be irritating and tiring if an attack continues.

TREATING HYSTERIA

Although this type of behavior may appear to be extreme, the affected person's feelings are very real to him or her. Hysteria is often a common and, some would argue, healthy response to situations of high stress.

1 Speak to the affected person firmly but quietly. Do not shout at her.

2 Move the person away from onlookers as subconsciously she may be reacting to the crowd.

3 Encourage the person to focus on breathing. If she is suffering from the effects of hyperventilation, such as cramps in the hands or dizziness, hand over a paper bag and advise her to re-breathe her own exhaled air.

4 Stay with the person until she has recovered.

5 Check the person for injury or any underlying medical condition, and treat as appropriate.

SIGNS AND SYMPTOMS OF HYSTERIA

- Screaming, shouting, and uncontrollable crying
- Hyperventilation (breathing too fast)— this may lead to dizziness and, or trembling
- An apparent inability to move (the person may appear to be rooted to the spot)
- Aggressive behavior (the person may direct this toward herself)

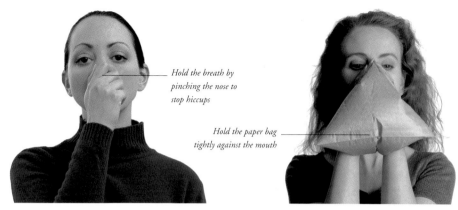

Hold the breath by
pinching the nose to
stop hiccups

Hold the paper bag
tightly against the mouth

Above
*Attacks of hiccups usually last for only a few minutes and
are not serious. There are many home remedies for treating
hiccups, such as holding the breath or drinking a glass of
water from the wrong side.*

Above
*To control hiccups or a panic attack, a person should breathe
in and out slowly into a paper bag 10 times then breathe
normally for another 10 breaths. This should be continued
until breathing is normal.*

TREATING HICCUPS

There are various suggested treatments
for hiccups.

● Give the affected person a paper bag
and encourage her to re-breathe her own
exhaled air.

● Make the person drink from the wrong side
of a cup.

● Tell the person to hold her breath for as long
as possible.

All these treatments work by increasing the
level of carbon dioxide in the blood, which
has a positive effect on breathing.

If hiccups persist for more than 30 minutes, or
the person is exhausted, seek medical advice.

PANIC ATTACKS

Panic attacks are sudden instances of
extreme anxiety accompanied by alarming
physical symptoms such as chest pains,
breathing problems, sweating, stomach
pains, palpitations (awareness of an
abnormally fast heartbeat), dizziness, and
faintness. The best way to treat this is to
encourage the sufferer to stay calm and to
remember that the attack will soon pass.
Rapid, shallow breathing can be helped by
breathing into a paper bag. Relaxation
exercises can help a person reduce anxiety
levels. If a person has frequent panic attacks,
she should see a doctor.

Allergies

An allergy is hypersensitivity to a substance (allergen) that is not normally considered to be harmful. The body's response can be mild but irritating or severe, quick, and life-threatening. The most extreme response is anaphylaxis, which can result in anaphylactic shock (see pages 50–51) that, if untreated, can kill. The number of allergy sufferers is increasing in the developed world.

TREATING MILD REACTIONS
Mild reactions usually involve skin irritation, minor swelling, and a rash. Some reactions take the form of red, irritated eyes and sneezing. If the sufferer shows signs of breathing difficulty or impaired consciousness, assume that the reaction is severe and call for immediate medical assistance.

Common allergens causing mild reactions include insects bites or stings, long grass, flowers, and long-haired animals.

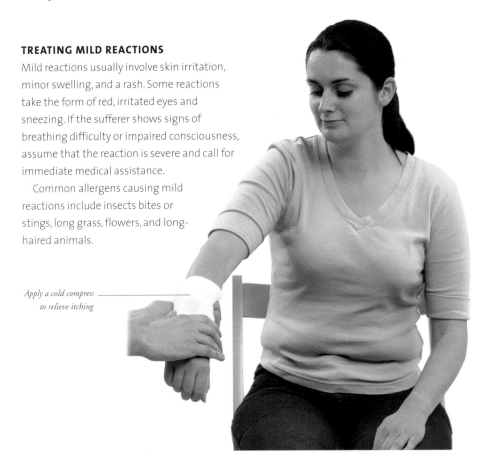

Apply a cold compress to relieve itching

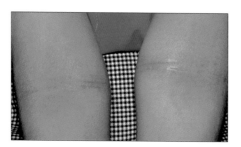

Left

Skin rashes that occur as a result of allergic reaction are often intensely itchy. Calamine lotion and oral antihistamines may help to relieve symptoms.

ALLERGIC RHINITIS, HAY FEVER, AND URTICARIA

If a person experiences an allergic reaction after inhaling a specific airborne substance, the membrane lining the nose, throat, and sinuses becomes inflamed, a condition termed allergic rhinitis. This increases mucus production and causes sinus congestion. Symptoms may include blocked or runny nose; itchy, red, watery eyes; sneezing; drowsiness; and a sore throat. Depending on the allergen, symptoms may be experienced year-round or seasonally, when the disorder is known as hay fever. Urticaria, also known as nettle rash or hives, is an intensely itchy rash that usually occurs as the result of an allergic reaction. The rash consists of white lumps and red, inflamed areas that may affect the whole body, and usually clears up after a few hours. Treatment for all these conditions depends on the use of antihistamines and avoiding the allergen when possible.

USING AN AUTO-INJECTOR

If you have been trained to do so, you may help somebody administer her own medication. Ensure that the medication belongs to the victim. Help her to expose an area of skin and to take the lid off the injector. Place the injector on the skin and help the victim push to administer the medication into her body.

1 Offer reassurance and find out if the person has a history of allergic reaction.

2 Apply a cold compress or calamine lotion to any rash or itchy skin.

3 Try to identify the source of the allergy so that it can be avoided. Reactions can become more extreme if the person is exposed to the same allergen in the future.

4 Seek medical advice because tests may be needed to identify the allergen.

Wilderness First Aid

What to Do if You are a Long Way from Help

Undertaking any journey into the wilderness requires careful preparation. When planning a trip you need to take many factors into account, including what you would do in the case of an accident or illness. Most treatments remain exactly the same for wilderness conditions.

PLANNING A JOURNEY The following are some of the things that you may like to consider when planning your journey, as well as some questions that you may like to ask yourself. Take a cellular phone but be aware that network coverage may be poor or nonexistent in the area you are visiting.

Location Is the area that you are visiting suitable for all the abilities in your family or group? An area with a reputation for beauty will not necessarily be safe.

Fitness Is everyone in your group fit enough to undertake the trip, or is anyone suffering from any injuries or illnesses? If so, does the person have enough medication?

The right clothes Having the right clothes for the environment that you will be visiting could mean the difference between life and death. Having an outer layer that is windproof, keeps water out, keeps the heat in, and allows sweat to evaporate will help the other layers stay dry and function correctly. The next layers should consist of a fleece-type jumper or jacket. A shirt and underwear made of polypropylene will draw moisture away from the skin. Today's modern clothing is designed to be functional even when wet and will dry out surprisingly quickly.

Footwear Choose footwear that supports your ankle, is waterproofed, and is comfortable and well worn in. This will help prevent sprains, broken bones, and blistering.

Equipment Carry first aid and survival equipment suitable for your route (see Wilderness First Aid Box, pages 236–237).

Planning your route Ensure that the route is realistically within the ability of your family or group and achievable in the amount of time available. Always tell someone who is not going with you what your route is, who is going, what time you are starting, and what time you will be finishing.

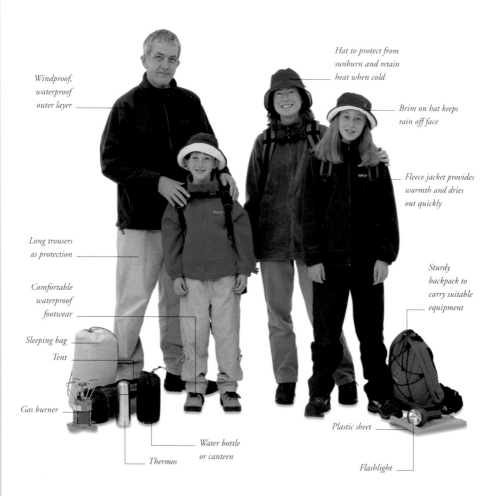

Windproof,
waterproof
outer layer

Hat to protect from
sunburn and retain
heat when cold

Brim on hat keeps
rain off face

Fleece jacket provides
warmth and dries
out quickly

Long trousers
as protection

Comfortable
waterproof
footwear

Sturdy
backpack to
carry suitable
equipment

Sleeping bag

Tent

Gas burner

Plastic sheet

Water bottle
or canteen

Thermos

Flashlight

IF FACED WITH A PROBLEM A LONG WAY FROM HELP If faced with an accident or illness a long way from help, your priorities are:

- To secure the safety of the whole group.
- To treat the injury or illness.
- To obtain help.
- To seek appropriate shelter.

Careful preparation is essential before you set off on your trip.

The biggest decision you will probably have to make relates to obtaining help. If you have not got a cellular phone, or you cannot get a signal, you will have to make alternative arrangements.

If one member of the group is unable to continue, a decision will have to be made to split the group or wait for help as a whole. The decision will depend on a number of factors:

- Popularity of the route and therefore likelihood of passers-by.
- Access to shelter.
- Nature of the injury or illness and the speed at which help is required.
- Skills of group members in survival and navigation.
- Weather conditions.
- Time of day.

If sending people for help, make sure that your equipment is divided appropriately. Ensure that those leaving have good directions and navigation aids and those remaining have sound shelter. If the weather is poor or it is dark, consider waiting until conditions improve. Instead, seek shelter.

Carrying an injured or ill person for help should be a last resort because it poses risks to both the person being carried and those lifting and moving him. There are a number of ways in which a stretcher can be improvized.

DIFFERENCES IN TREATMENT Since you are likely to be in wilderness conditions for some time, the following should be considered:

- Maintaining warmth when treating shock (see pages 44–45) or conditions such as hypothermia (see pages 136–137) may require the creation of shelter. Focus on putting blankets or survival bags under the injured person and covering the head, hands, and feet as well as putting a blanket over him.
- Consider shelter from the sun and the heat and make sure that everyone in the party drinks enough liquid, including the injured person (providing that he is fully conscious).
- Be aware that altitude sickness may develop if you are high in the mountains because of reduced levels of oxygen in the air. Symptoms include tiredness, headache, unsteadiness, and nausea.
- Broken bones, burns, and contusions swell. Continually recheck bandaging to ensure that it is not cutting off circulation. Loosen and re-tie as necessary.
- Consider providing extra bandaging support to broken bones—particularly if the injured person needs to be moved.

Wilderness First Aid

Should there be an accident, or a member of your group is taken ill, you have two choices: either send someone for help or wait for help to arrive. The decision you make will depend on the weather conditions, the ability to navigate, how far it is to get help, and what kind of terrain you will have to cover. Only in the most extreme circumstances should a victim be left alone, and you should leave the injured person spare clothing and food. The victim will also require a whistle and/or flashlight in order to alert the rescue services. Finally, the person should be told to stay where he is and not move.

GETTING HELP Whoever goes for help should carry with them enough spare clothing and equipment to deal with any situation that may be faced. The person should also take the following information:

● The exact location of the injured person or group (this is best done using a six-figure grid reference).

● What has happened.
● When it occurred.
● What injuries or condition they have.
● A description of where they are.
● Who else is with them.

ATTRACTING HELP There are internationally recognized signals that can be used while out in the wilderness that are easily remembered and require no special equipment. Although shouting for help may attract attention, after a while you will become hoarse and tired. Voices do not carry as well as other sounds such as whistle blasts, which can be heard over surprisingly large distances. At night, light can also travel much further than voices and during the day a reflective

Six whistle blasts are a recognized signal for help

Leave a flashlight so the victim can signal for help

object such as a mirror can send the rays of the sun a considerable distance.

There are two international signals for help. The first is SOS, which represents the phrase Save Our Souls. Although Morse code is no longer used in everyday life, it is still practised to summon help in emergency situations. For an audible signal on a whistle, give three short blasts (S) three long blasts (O) and three short blasts (S). With a light signal, give three short flashes (S) three long flashes (O) and three short flashes (S). Alternatively, six blasts of a whistle or six flashes of light in quick succession also mean that help is needed. A red flare also acts as an emergency distress call on water and in the mountains.

Use a flashlight to flash an SOS signal to attract help

COMMUNICATING WITH THE RESCUE TEAMS

You may find that you can hear instructions given by a mountain rescue team or similar through a megaphone from a helicopter but are unable to shout back to them.

There are three ways in which you can communicate that you understood their message:

- Give three blasts on a whistle in quick succession, repeated after a 1-minute interval.
- Give three flashes of the flashlight in quick succession, repeated after a 1-minute interval
- Send up a white flare.

Avalanche and Snow Survival Techniques

Over the years, remote and faraway places have become more accessible and, although as much care as possible is taken whenever there is snow on a mountain or slope, an avalanche is always possible. Find out the local emergency signals for "avalanche warning" and "avalanche imminent" and heed them. Many avalanches are caused by a skier going off-course or ignoring local warnings. Make sure that you are wearing appropriate clothing for the mountain and that you have at least a whistle as a rescue aid. Leave details of your route with a local contact.

SURVIVING AN AVALANCHE If caught in an avalanche, try to hold on to an immovable object for as long as you can as the more snow that passes you, the less likely you are to be buried when it comes to a halt.

If at all possible, try to work your way to the side of the flow by using a swimming or rolling motion, keep your mouth shut, and try to cover your mouth and nose with the top of your sweater or parka while continuing the

Above
Holding on to an immovable object such as a tree when caught in an avalanche will increase your chances of survival because you are less likely to be buried by snow.

Above
Use a swimming or rolling motion to try to work your way to the side of the snow fall. Try to cover your mouth and nose with your jacket, scarf, or sweater to prevent inhaling snow.

Above
When you stop, make an air space for yourself by folding your arms in front of your face and chest. Move one hand upward and try to dig your way out if you can feel air.

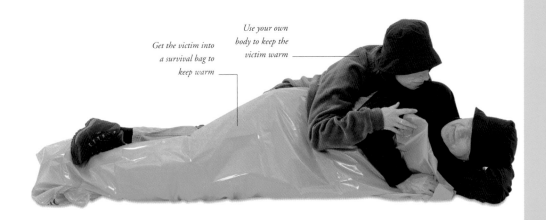

Get the victim into a survival bag to keep warm

Use your own body to keep the victim warm

swimming motion. When you come to a stop, create an air space by folding your arms in front of your face and chest while the snow comes to a halt. Orientate yourself by spitting and feeling which way it falls. Try to move one hand upward and if you feel air, and you are able to, dig your way out. Otherwise, conserve both your air and your energy until help arrives.

There are various avalanche beacons. These are small, portable transceivers, which are a worthwhile investment for those regularly spending time in the mountains.

HYPOTHERMIA Hypothermia is the lowering of the body's core temperature to 95°F or below. The best treatment for hypothermia is prevention. As the body's temperature drops there may be signs and symptoms that, if recognized early enough, can prevent an easily treatable condition becoming fatal. In the outdoors it is important to watch out for these signs in the group that you are with and to

take early action to prevent deterioration. For more information on hypothermia, see pages 136–137.

TREATMENT

Once recognized, the treatment for hypothermia is to rewarm the victim to the body's natural temperature. However, this needs to be done with care because rough handling could lead to a heart attack in some people.

1 Try to provide a warm, dry environment. Lay the person at risk down, ensuring that he is insulated from the ground, and gently remove any wet items of clothing, replacing them with dry ones as you go. Since we lose almost a third of our body heat through our heads, this should be covered as quickly as possible. If the person is able, sips of a warm drink may be taken, although this should not be relied upon and other warming techniques will need to be employed.

SIGNS AND SYMPTOMS OF DESCENT INTO HYPOTHERMIA

Core body temperature	Sign/symptom
96.8°F	Sensation of cold, stumbling, personality changes, mild confusion
95°F	Slurred speech, poor coordination, no memory of events (on recovery)
91.4°F	Shivering disappears and is replaced by stiff muscles
87.8°F	Pupils become dilated, loss of consciousness
86°F	Unconsciousness
84.2°F	Muscle stiffness disappears
73.4°F	Breathing stops
64.4°F	Death

2 Try to get the victim into a sleeping or survival bag and cuddle up close, reassuring him all the time. Closely monitor the victim's progress by continuing to talk to him, noting any changes in the level of consciousness (see pages 61–63).

3 Although space blankets or silver foil blankets are useful when used with other equipment, they work by reflecting the person's own body heat. If the victim is cold, they will reflect the cold, making the situation worse. They should therefore never be relied upon on their own.

4 If you have a tent or survival shelter available, set this up and get inside as soon as possible. Take care to ensure that other members of your group do not succumb to the cold.

Cold Water Survival Techniques

Today there are many different pursuits that can be undertaken on water, often by people with limited experience. Under appropriate supervision most water sports are perfectly safe, although the combination of weather, unpredictable water, and inexperience can lead to difficulties. The biggest danger from the water is drowning. There are simple measures that can help prevent this situation, such as wearing a personal flotation device or having rescue equipment to hand.

IN THE WATER ALONE

Should an accident occur and you find yourself in a situation where you may be in water for some time, there are some simple but effective ways of staying as warm as possible.

Cover your head with a hat or hood—remember that one-third of your body heat is lost through your head

Blasts on a whistle, or the release of flares, will alert others to your situation

Bring your knees up to your chest and wrap your arms around them, making yourself into a ball. This exposes less skin area to the water, which slows down the cooling process and buys you valuable time

COLD SHOCK

Falling into cold water can almost literally take your breath away. This is known as cold shock. The body's response to this sudden immersion in cold water causes the breathing and heart rate to soar. Although this is normally not a problem, when the water is less than 59°F, sudden immersion can cause the heart to beat at rates of 150–180 beats per minute and the breathing rate to rise to 60–90 breaths per minute. This may completely incapacitate a young fit person, and in a less fit or older person cause heart attack or stroke.

When safely out of the water, treat the victim for hypothermia (see pages 136–137) and call 911. Monitor and maintain the airway (see pages 12–17) and be prepared to resuscitate the victim (see pages 29–33) if necessary.

IN THE WATER AS A GROUP

If there is more than one person in the water then there are additional steps.

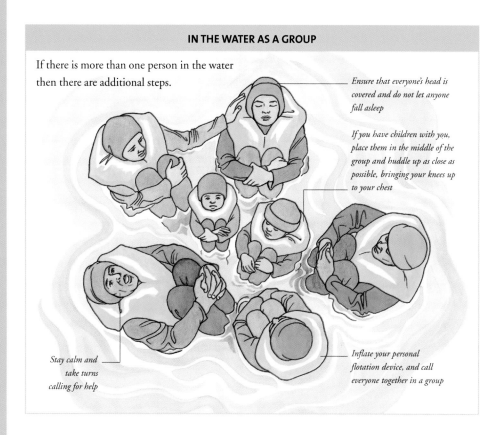

Ensure that everyone's head is covered and do not let anyone fall asleep

If you have children with you, place them in the middle of the group and huddle up as close as possible, bringing your knees up to your chest

Stay calm and take turns calling for help

Inflate your personal flotation device, and call everyone together in a group

PREPARING FOR ACTIVITY WHERE IMMERSION IN COLD WATER IS A POSSIBILITY The temperature of the coastal waters around the US can be as cold as 40°F or as warm as 80°F, making even the warmest ocean temperature 18 degrees cooler than our body temperature (98.6°F). Water conducts heat approximately 25 times faster than air, meaning that heat will be lost rapidly from the body. Hypothermia is therefore a big risk following immersion in cold water, particularly if you are not wearing appropriate clothing. If you know that there is a risk that you will be immersed in water for some time, always wear proper protective clothing such as nylon underwear, a thick layer of fleece, a dry suit, and a head covering.

Always undertake water sports under appropriate supervision and consider the many sources of information about the conditions of the water that you are visiting, such as the coastguard, beach offices, sailing and diving clubs, and local water-sports shops.

Stretcher Improvization

In certain extreme circumstances it may be necessary to transport a person who is sick or injured to a place of safety. Should you find yourself in such a situation, there are a number of techniques whereby a stretcher can be quickly improvized.

METHOD 1: BRANCH AND CLOTHING

1 Select two strong branches that will extend by about 1 foot either end of the person to be carried. Ensure that the branch is tested for rot and that any sharp parts are cut away. It is also worth checking for moss at each end as this will make any grip slippery. Although the branches do not have to be exactly the same size, it will obviously help if they are roughly the same length. It is vital that they are capable of holding the weight of the victim.

2 Now select some clothing that is strong since this will bear the weight of the victim. Items made of denim and good quality cotton T-shirts are ideal. You should not forget yourself—do not give away clothing that may mean you are at risk from the weather.

3 Slide the clothing on to the poles with the poles coming through the arms of the garment. Place the next piece of clothing on to the poles in the same way and overlap the first item. Place enough pieces of clothing on to the poles to ensure that the victim's head and legs will be supported.

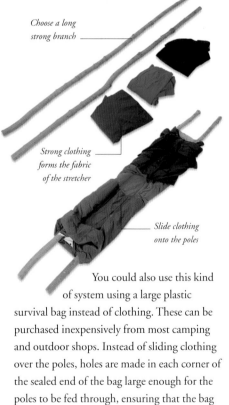

Choose a long strong branch

Strong clothing forms the fabric of the stretcher

Slide clothing onto the poles

You could also use this kind of system using a large plastic survival bag instead of clothing. These can be purchased inexpensively from most camping and outdoor shops. Instead of sliding clothing over the poles, holes are made in each corner of the sealed end of the bag large enough for the poles to be fed through, ensuring that the bag will not split once any weight is placed on it.

METHOD 2: CARRYING A SURVIVAL BAG

1 It is possible to use the survival bag as a stretcher without damaging it. Lay the bag out and, depending on how many people you have to help with the carry, collect stones large enough for each person to grip. Next, using string or rope, tie the stones at each corner of the bag and at each side in the middle. If stones are not available, items of clothing such as hats, socks, or gloves can be used in their place.

2 There are definite limitations to this kind of stretcher. The polythene is relatively easy to split, especially on rough ground, and when wet can be extremely slippery. Therefore care should be taken when picking the stretcher up and you should always take things slowly.

3 If you do not have a survival bag handy, the flysheet of a tent will do instead. However, bear in mind that rocks and stones may damage the fabric.

Lay the survival bag flat on the ground to use as a stretcher

Find several stones large enough to be gripped and tie them inside to help carry the bag

Wrap the ends of the survival bag around the stones to form handholds

Loading and Carrying a Stretcher

Consider carefully whether the benefits of moving somebody will outweigh the risks. If you are able to seek appropriate shelter and send or call for help, it is generally considered safer to stay where you are, particularly at night or if the weather is bad. Alongside the danger of getting lost or falling, carrying a stretcher comes with the risk of damaging the backs of those carrying it.

PREPARATION FOR LOADING AND CARRYING

Consider the following:

● Have you got enough people to lift the victim safely onto the stretcher?

● What are the conditions of the ground underneath your feet? Are you liable to slip or sink, or is it on a steep slope? Will the ground move?

● Does everyone involved understand what you are doing and how you are planning to do it?

● Do you or anyone else in your party have any injuries or conditions that could be greatly worsened by the lift?

● Are there any other factors that may hinder or prevent you from safely carrying out the lift?

Try to eliminate or reduce any of the conditions that the answers to these questions identify as a risk. If in doubt, do not attempt to lift the stretcher and seek shelter while waiting for help to arrive.

GETTING A PERSON ON TO THE STRETCHER

It may be possible for you to lift the person directly onto the stretcher. Ideally this should

be done with a minimum of two people. Bring the stretcher to the victim and lay it down as close as you can without it being in your way. Decide who will take the top half and who will take the bottom half of the person to be lifted.

1 Sit the person up and ask her to cross or fold her arms across her chest.

2 Squatting behind the victim, slide your hands under her arms, taking hold of her wrists or lower arms.

3 Ask your partner to squat beside the victim and pass their arms under her thighs, taking hold of the legs.

4 The person at the head end takes control and will determine the timing of the lift. When ready, working together and keeping your backs straight, rise slowly and move the victim onto the stretcher.

SURVIVAL BAG/FLYSHEET TECHNIQUE If you are using the survival bag/flysheet technique, it will be easier to put the stretcher underneath the victim before you add the poles. The easiest way for this to be done is to use one of two methods:

Method 1

Lay the bag/flysheet next to the victim and gather up approximately half of the fabric on the side closest to her, placing it as close as you can to body. Turn the victim onto her side and place the bundle as close as you can to her body, then and gently roll her back. Now pull the remainder of the bag/sheet out from the sides. You are then ready to add the poles.

Method 2

Concertina-fold the top and bottom ends of the bag toward the center with one person on each side of the victim, placing the folded bag/sheet under the hollow in the small of her back (if you need more room you can gently lift her hips). Together, pull the bottom part down toward the victim's feet and then the other half of the bag/sheet can be pulled up toward her head. You can then add the poles.

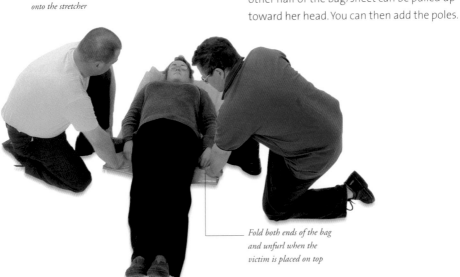

Turn the victim on to her side and roll her onto the stretcher

Fold both ends of the bag and unfurl when the victim is placed on top

LIFTING

The following principles will reduce your risk of injury when performing any lift or moving and handling.

1 Stand with your feet shoulder-width apart, with one foot slightly in front of the other.

2 Bend at your hips and your knees, not at your back. Keep your back straight but not rigid.

3 Get a secure grip of the stretcher. Raise your head.

4 Use your strongest muscles (in your thighs) to lift, keeping your elbows close to your body.

One person should take the lead at all times—usually the person guiding the head. Take regular breaks as needed and move slowly and carefully.

Keep your back straight when lifting a stretcher

One- and Two-Person Carries

If moving an injured or ill person is absolutely necessary, encouraging him to move by himself is by far the best approach, minimizing risk to both you and him. However, this is not always possible. There are a number of dangers inherent in lifting and moving people and the task should not be undertaken lightly. The following techniques require no real equipment and in an emergency situation can be very effective.

ONE-PERSON CARRIES

The human crutch

If you find yourself in a situation where the injured person has, for instance, sprained an ankle and is having difficulty in walking, this technique will provide additional support if nothing else, such as a walking stick or crutch, is available.

1 Stand on the person's injured or affected side, pass her arm around your neck and grasp her hand or wrist.

2 Place your other arm around her waist and grasp her clothes, preferably the top of the trousers or a belt.

3 Move off with your inside foot first, walking at the victim's pace.

Piggy back

Although this is an effective carry, how far you will be physically capable of moving the victim will depend on her size and weight. It also reduces your ability to carry your own equipment, particularly if you are hiking with backpacks.

1 Crouch in front of the victim with your back toward her and ask her to put her arms over your shoulders.

2 Grasp the victim's thighs, pull them in toward you and slowly stand up, remembering to keep your back straight.

The drag

This technique is really for extreme emergencies and will be effective only over short distances as it is very labor-intensive. Its key use is in moving people from very hazardous areas quickly.

1 Crouch behind the victim. Carefully pull him toward you. Stop, take a step back, and pull the victim toward you again.

2 Repeat this procedure until you have reached your destination.

TWO-PERSON CARRIES

It is far easier for two people to control and move someone. However, these techniques do have their limitations, even with two people, and require a little practise.

Two-handed seat carry

1 Crouch down, facing each other on either side of the injured person.

2 Cross over your arms behind the victim and grab hold of her waistband or belt.

Cross arms and grab waistband

3 Pass your other hands under the victim's knees and grasp each other's wrists.

Pass other hands under knees and grasp wrists

FOUR-HANDED SEAT CARRY

The two-handed and, in particular, the four-handed seat carries can only be used with conscious people because they require the person being carried to have some control over her body and give some assistance to the rescuers.

1 With the person to be carried standing close to you, first hold your left wrist with your right hand, and ask your carrying partner to do the same.

2 Now link hands, taking hold of your partner's right wrist. This should form a square.

3 Allow the victim to gently sit back onto your hands and get her to place her hands around your shoulders.

It should be noted that this is extremely strenuous and awkward for the rescuers.

4 Bring your hands toward the middle of the victim's thighs.

5 Get in close to the injured person and stand up slowly; you are now ready to move off.

Helicopter Rescue

Helicopters have saved many lives since their introduction as a rescue tool. As well as being used to evacuate people from ships and mountains and rescue people from the sea, they are being utilized by numerous ambulance services all over the US to transport seriously ill or injured people to the hospital. Although they are an effective life-saving tool, they can also be extremely dangerous if safety precautions are not followed. Should you find yourself in a situation where you or a member of your group is to be rescued by helicopter, the following simple precautions should be taken.

Wave your arms to attract the crew's attention

Keep dogs and children under control

1 The pilot will select the best area for the helicopter to land but if there is an obvious clear area that you believe they may wish to use, try to clear it of any obstructions such as loose debris. Assemble everybody to the windward of the landing site, as the helicopter will approach into the wind. You must be at least 165 feet away from the landing point.

Left
Gather together everyone who is to be rescued and assemble windward of the landing site because the helicopter will approach into the wind.

SEARCH AND RESCUE

In addition to the fire, police, and ambulance emergency services, a number of specialist organizations exist in the US that operate search and rescue services in more hostile conditions.

Search and rescue units operate in all areas of the country, providing an emergency service to anyone lost or injured in remote wilderness areas such as mountains or forests. These highly trained volunteers work in cooperation with the authorities and they are well-equipped with specialist vehicles, helicopters, and medical resources. On call 24 hours a day, they are contacted through the usual emergency agencies.

Emergencies at sea are dealt with by the US Coastguard and Lifeboat services. In addition to participating in search and rescue operations, these organizations run public education programs, carry out vessel safety checks, and are involved in environmental protection. The United States Coastguard Auxiliary is a nationwide force of more than 35,000 volunteers specially trained to form a vital part of the Coastguard.

To summon any rescue service you should phone 911.

2 If it is not obvious where you are, wave some bright clothing or shine a flashlight so that the pilot and crew can see you. While the helicopter lands, stay still, holding on to any loose items of clothing or baggage. If you are on the beach you may find it more comfortable to cover your face because of the downdraft caused by the aircraft, which will stir up the sand.

3 Once the helicopter has landed, under no circumstances approach it until you are signaled to do so by the pilot. When you are told to move toward the aircraft, approach in the direction that is indicated by the pilot. This will normally be from the front and to the pilot's right-hand side. This is so that you remain in the pilot's sight at all times. Follow any instructions you are given by the crew exactly.

RESCUE BY WINCH If you are being rescued from a winch, for example, you are being taken off a boat, do not touch the winch lines until they have reached the ground as they carry a static electrical charge until they have been earthed.

Equipment, Medicines, and Complementary Medicine

Using Dressings and Cold Compresses

A dressing is a piece of material that covers a wound to protect it from infection or to staunch bleeding. Cold compresses are used to reduce swelling and relieve pain. They are particularly useful for sprains and strains.

COLD COMPRESSES There are three main types of cold compress:

- Ice pack
- Cold pad
- Chemical pack

Applying an ice pack

Do not apply ice directly to the skin.

1 Wrap a bag of crushed ice in a clean piece of material such as a triangular bandage or tea towel.

2 Apply to the injured part for up to 20 minutes, securing in place as necessary.

3 Replace the ice as needed. Items from the freezer, such as frozen peas, make a good alternative to crushed ice.

Applying a cold pad

1 Soak a pad such as a washcloth or folded triangular bandage in cold water. Wring it out so that it does not drip.

2 Apply to the injured area for up to 20 minutes, securing as necessary.

3 Wet the pad as needed to keep it cool.

4 If the wound is bleeding, tie the bandage firmly directly over the site of the injury to ensure maximum pressure.

5 Check the circulation below the site of the bandaging (see page 95).

Using chemical packs Cool packs are available from most pharmacies or sports shops. They contain chemicals which, when mixed together by tapping or twisting the surrounding plastic bag, become cold. The pad can then be used in the same way as an ice pack.

1 Follow the instructions on the pack.

2 If the pack is damaged, do not use it because the chemicals may leak onto the skin. Chemical packs are ideal for situations in which you may be some distance from water or ice.

APPLYING A DRESSING

1 Remove the wrapping, taking care not to touch the dressing. Place the dressing gently over the wound.

2 Wind the bandage around the dressing, covering the entire pad.

3 Secure the bandage in place with tape, a bow, or a square knot.

WHEN USING DRESSINGS

- The dressing should be larger than the area that is being treated.
- Place non-adhesive dressings shiny side down.
- If blood comes through the dressing, do not remove it. Place another dressing on top of it.
- For larger wounds or for large burns, use additional layers of padding on top of the dressing.
- Check that the seal on a prepacked dressing is not broken; a broken seal means that the dressing is no longer sterile.

Check that the bandage is secure but not too tight

To reduce the risk of infection

- Wash your hands and wear gloves if possible.
- Open the dressing as close to the wound as possible.
- Do not touch the wound or the dressing.

IMPROVIZED DRESSINGS

If you do not have a prepacked dressing available, use a piece of clean, non-fluffy material such as a clean handkerchief, a freshly washed pillow case for burns covering a large surface area, or a clean plastic sandwich bag or piece of plastic wrap for smaller burns.

TYPES OF DRESSING

There are various prepacked varieties of dressing available:

Non-adhesive These usually have one shiny side made of a material that minimizes the risk of the dressing sticking to the wound. Generally more expensive than ordinary dressings, they are good for burns and scrapes.

Gauze These may be backed by a layer of cotton padding. Gauze pads come in various sizes. The larger ones are particularly useful for managing wounds that are bleeding profusely.

Adhesive bandages These are available in a variety of sizes and are used for smaller cuts. There are specially shaped bandages for fingers, heels, and elbows, decorative bandages for children; and colored bandages for a range of skin tones. To ensure maximum cleanliness, use individually wrapped bandages rather than cutting one from a long roll.

HOLDING DRESSINGS IN PLACE

Dressings can be held in place:
- With a bandage—either one attached to the dressing or a separate one. Triangular, tubular, and Ace bandages can all be used to hold dressings in place.
- With tape—take care not to stick tape to the wound. Do not tape all the way around a limb because this may damage circulation.
- By the injured person—injuries to the face,

for example, are particularly hard to bandage and the dressing may be better held in place by hand.

If using tape (or an adhesive bandage) ask the injured person if he or she is aware of any allergy to latex. If there is a history of allergy, use an alternative method of securing the dressing.

Bandaging

Bandages have three key uses: applying pressure to bleeding wounds; covering wounds and burns; and providing support and immobilization for broken bones, sprains, and strains. The three main types are triangular, Ace, and tubular.

TYPES OF BANDAGE

Triangular bandages Made from cloth or from paper, these are exceptionally versatile. When they are made into a pad they can be used as a cold compress or for padding. When folded up they can be used to provide support or pressure; when unfolded they can be used as a support sling or cover bandage.

Ace bandages Used to provide support or secure dressings in place.

Tubular bandages Larger ones are used to support joints or hold dressings in place, smaller tubular bandages are ideal for finger injuries.

General principles of bandaging

1 Work with the injured person, explaining what you are doing.

2 Work in front of the injured person where possible and from the injured side if you can.

3 Bandage firmly over bleeding and securely over broken bones, but not so tight as to compromise circulation below the site of the injury.

4 When wrapping bandages around an injured person, use the body's natural hollows such as the knees, ankles, neck, and small of the back to slide the bandages gently into place.

5 Be aware that most injuries swell—check regularly to ensure that the bandage is still comfortable. Also, check that the bandage remains firmly secured, particularly if the injured person has to move, as movement can loosen the bandage.

6 Secure bandages with tape, clips, a bow, or a square knot.

7 Make sure that bandages, especially knots, do not press into the skin. Place padding between the bandaging and the skin as necessary.

TRIANGULAR BANDAGES These are amongst the most versatile of all items of first aid equipment. Usually made of washable cotton, they are also available in a disposable paper form. In its open form, a triangular bandage can be used as a sling or as a cover bandage.

TO USE AS A COLD COMPRESS OR PADDING OR TO APPLY PRESSURE WITH A DRESSING

1 Use a narrow fold bandage.

2 Fold the two ends into the middle.

3 Keep folding the ends into the middle until the size is appropriate for use. Bandages are best stored in this way in a plastic bag in a dry place.

USING A TRIANGULAR BANDAGE

Making a broad fold to support broken bones or hold dressings loosely in place

1 To make a broad fold, fold the point to the base of the bandage.

2 Fold the bandage in half again. This is a broad fold.

Making a narrow fold to control bleeding

1 To make a narrow fold, fold a broad fold in half again. This is a narrow fold.

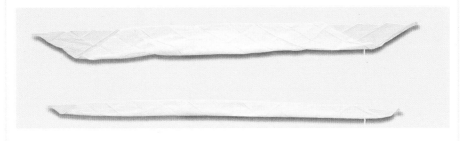

TYING A SQUARE KNOT

When you tie a bandage, it is best to do so with a square knot. Square knots lie flat, so they do not press into the injured person, and they are easy to untie. Alternative fastenings include tying a bow, using a pin, securing with tape, or using a clip.

1 Pass the right end of the bandage over the left and tuck it under.

2 Bring both ends alongside each other.

3 Pass the left end over the right and tuck it under.

4 Pull both ends firmly to complete the knot.

FOOT COVER BANDAGE

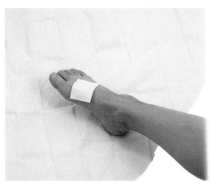

1 Fold a hem along the base of the triangular bandage. Place the victim's foot on the bandage and bring the point down toward the victim's ankle.

2 Fold the bandage up over the foot.

3 Fold the two ends of the bandage around the ankle and tie loosely.

4 Pull the point of the bandage over the knot and tuck it away. The victim may find it comfortable to have the foot in an elevation sling.

ACE BANDAGES Ace bandages are used to secure dressings or to provide support, particularly to sprains and strains. They are usually made of cotton, gauze, or linen and are secured in place with pins or tape.

TYPES OF ACE BANDAGE There are three key types of Ace bandage, as pictured right:

Ace bandages come in a variety of sizes. For an adult, the following are the recommended widths for different parts of the body:

Finger: ½ inch;
Hand: 1 inch;
Arm: 1½–2 inches;
Leg: 2–3 inches

Conforming
Used for securing dressings and providing support

Crepe
Used for support, particularly for joint sprains

Open-weave
Best used for applying light dressings

HOW TO APPLY AN ACE BANDAGE

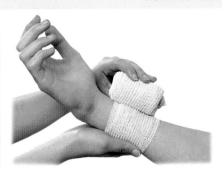

1 Partly unroll the bandage.

2 Place the unrolled end below the injury and do two complete turns around the limb to secure the bandage in place.

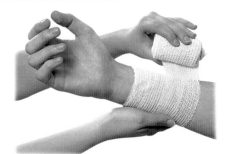

3 Bandage up the limb, using spiral turns. Be aware that conforming and crepe bandages mold to the shape of the body and while they should be applied firmly, take care not to over-stretch the bandage as this may impair circulation.

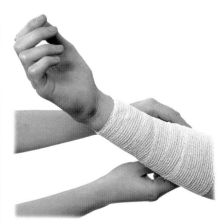

4 Finish off with a single turn and secure in place. Secure with tape, clip, or by tying off.

5 To tie off an Ace bandage, leave enough length to do two complete turns of the limb. Cut down the middle of the bandage. Tie a knot at the bottom of the split and place both ends around the limb, one in each direction. Tie them in a bow or a square knot.

APPLYING TUBULAR GAUZE

These bandages come in several sizes. The smallest size is used to hold dressings on to fingers and toes. It comes with its own applicator and is best secured with tape.

1 Cut two and half times the length of the finger or toe to be bandaged and push all of this on to the applicator.

2 Place the dressing over the wound. Slide the applicator over the finger or toe.

3 Hold the gauze at the base of the finger or toe and pull the applicator upward, covering the finger or toe with one layer of gauze.

4 Above the finger or toe, twist the applicator twice and then push it back down, covering the finger or toe with another layer of gauze.

5 Tape the gauze in place.

SIGNS AND SYMPTOMS OF REDUCED CIRCULATION

- Pale skin, becoming blue
- Skin feeling cold to the touch
- Injured person complains of tingling or loss of feeling
- Weak or slow pulse in an injured limb
- Slow capillary refill below the site of the bandage (see below)

1 Look and feel for the signs and symptoms of reduced circulation. When bandaging, leave an area of skin exposed below the site of the injury to enable regular checks of circulation.

2 Ask the injured person to report any tingling or loss of feeling.

3 Gently squeeze the skin or the nail bed below the site of the injury and bandaging until the color disappears from the skin. When pressure is released, the color should return swiftly (color returns as the small blood vessels, the capillaries, refill with blood). If color does not return quickly, circulation may be restricted.

If there are signs that circulation is restricted, gently loosen the bandage(s). If the bandage is covering a wound or burn, do not remove dressings. If it is supporting a broken bone, take care to support the injury as you loosen and re-tie the bandage.

CHECKING CIRCULATION

Bandages can cut off circulation, particularly as the injury swells. Check circulation below the site of the bandaging immediately after treatment and every 10 minutes thereafter.

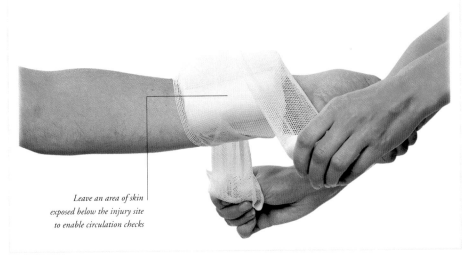

Leave an area of skin exposed below the injury site to enable circulation checks

First Aid Kit for the Home

Most pharmacies and major supermarkets supply ready-made first aid kits for the home.
Alternatively, you may wish to put together your own first aid kit to best meet the needs of
your family.

STORING FIRST AID EQUIPMENT The equipment should be stored in a clearly labeled waterproof box in an easy-to-access position. The American symbol for first aid is a red cross on a white background.

WHAT SHOULD BE IN THE KIT? Consider carefully the needs that you might have in the home for first aid equipment. Your kit should be able to provide you with equipment to do the following tasks:

- Manage heavy bleeding
- Cover minor wounds and burns
- Clean small cuts and scrapes
- Provide support for strains, sprains, and broken bones
- Provide cover for large burns
- Apply a cold compress

In addition, you may want to store over-the-counter remedies with your kit, such as analgesics and extra family medications.
Numbers of each item will be influenced by the number, age, and activities of people in the home. Very young children, for example, will have lots of small bumps and scrapes and will therefore benefit from a copious supply of brightly colored bandages. Sports-minded teenagers or adults may be more at risk of sprains and strains.

POTENTIAL EQUIPMENT

Small, medium, and large dressings
These are sterile pads with bandages attached that can be used to control heavy bleeding and cover minor wounds. See also pages 220–222.

Triangular bandages
These are an extremely versatile piece of equipment. Folded into a pad, they can be used as a cold compress or as padding around a painful area. They can provide cover for burns or large scrapes and support broken bones. See also Triangular Bandages, pages 224–225.

Adhesive bandages
For small wounds.

Non-adhesive sterile dressings (various sizes), safety tape, adhesive tape, and hypoallergenic tape
Dressings can be cut to size and used to cover scrapes, burns, and small wounds.

Gauze swabs
For use with water to clean wounds.

Ace bandages, compression bandages, tubular bandages
For use in providing support to sprains and strains. See also page 223 and pages 228–229.

Disposable gloves
For use in managing body fluids.

Blunt-ended scissors

Tweezers

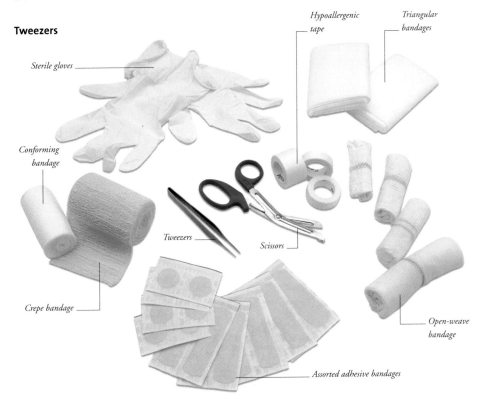

Hypoallergenic tape

Triangular bandages

Sterile gloves

Conforming bandage

Tweezers

Scissors

Crepe bandage

Open-weave bandage

Assorted adhesive bandages

First Aid Kit for the Car

More than 40,000 people are killed on the roads in the US each year, with thousands of accidents every day. Carrying simple first aid equipment in your car can help to protect you at the scene of an accident and provide you with the tools to carry out necessary first aid procedures. In addition, a well-stocked first aid kit can provide many items needed to ensure comfort on long journeys.

PROTECTING YOURSELF Many people are injured while helping at the scene of a road accident. If you stop to help, make sure that you are clearly visible to oncoming traffic. Use your car as a warning signal and consider carrying a combination of the following equipment:

- Hazard warning triangle
- High visibility jacket or strap
- Flashlight

KEEPING THE INJURED PERSON WARM
- Blanket(s)

There may be little that you can do for many seriously injured victims other than treat for shock (see pages 44–45). Keeping the person warm is an important part of this treatment and can be potentially life-saving. Carry at least one blanket in your car. In addition to its value in treating shock, it can also be used as padding for broken bones or to keep family members warm if your car breaks down in freezing conditions.

TREATING INJURIES Space is often in short supply in the boot of a car so a first aid kit should be kept to the minimum. The following provides a basic guide for a car first aid kit:

- 4 assorted sterile dressings: small, medium, and large
- 2 triangular bandages
- Adhesive bandages or non-adhesive dressings and hypoallergenic tape
- Gloves and face shield
- Notepad and pen

FAMILY JOURNEYS In addition to carrying equipment for major emergencies, you may wish to include useful items for family travels.

These include:
- Emesis bags
- Moist towelettes or baby wipes
- Alcohol wipes (when water is not available)
- Cold pads (these are cold compress ice packs made from chemicals that get cold when you break the seal; see also page 220)

● Over-the-counter remedies such as acetaminophen for common ailments

STORING YOUR FIRST AID KIT If storing your first aid kit in the main part of the car, ensure that it is either made of a soft material or that it is firmly bolted down to prevent it becoming a dangerous missile if the car stops suddenly. The container should be waterproof and clearly labeled.

ON A BOAT

The guidance for cars applies equally well to boats. In addition, boat first aid kits may include:

● Strong pliers for cutting away fish hooks
● Treatments for common marine animal bites and stings
● Suncream and relief for sunburn
● Medication for crew members

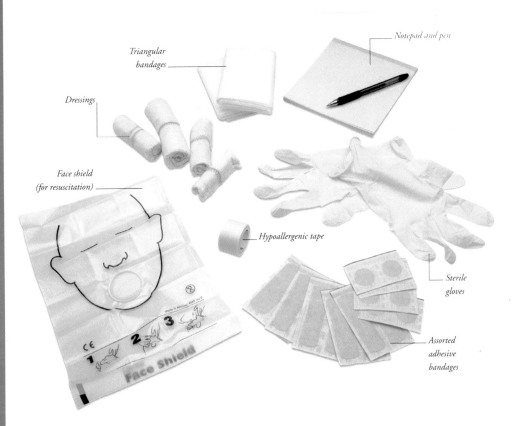

Triangular bandages

Notepad and pen

Dressings

Face shield (for resuscitation)

Hypoallergenic tape

Sterile gloves

Assorted adhesive bandages

Wilderness First Aid Kit

If planning a journey away from towns and easy access to medical treatment, consider carefully what equipment to take with you. Since you will be carrying the first aid kit yourself it should contain lightweight essential supplies. If you will be in wild country with a guide, check what equipment will be brought for the group (guides often have extended training in emergency skills) and what items you should bring personally.

KEEPING WARM AND PROVIDING SHELTER
This is often the first priority for an injured person in a wilderness situation. Useful equipment includes:

● Survival bags: tough polythene body-size bags that can be used as protection from the elements. Often brightly colored, they are also a useful signaling tool
● Sleeping bag/tent/floor mat
● Complete spare set of clothes
● Method of warming up hot drinks or food

SIGNALING FOR HELP If an accident happens, the best advice is usually to stay put and call for help. Consider taking a combination of the following:

● Cellular phone (but check network coverage in the area that you are going to be in)
● Whistle
● Mirror
● Flashlight
● Rescue flare

PROTECTION FROM THE ELEMENTS AND WILDLIFE When shelter is limited and you are exerting yourself walking, both heatstroke and heat exhaustion are real risks (see pages 139–140). Keep your head covered and wear cool clothes that allow sweat to evaporate from the body. Drink regularly and try and keep out of the sun during its hottest time (around midday). Remember too that insect and animal bites are common.

The following may be useful additions to your kit:

● Insect repellent
● Over-the-counter remedy for insect stings
● Sunscreen and sunburn remedy
● Sunglasses

TREATING INJURIES Restrict first aid equipment to a minimum to keep weight down.

The following should cover most key emergency situations:

● 4 assorted sterile dressings: small, medium, and large

● 2 triangular bandages

● Adhesive bandages or non-adhesive dressings and hypoallergenic tape

● Conforming bandages to fit ankles and knees (this bandage may enable a person with a sprained ankle to carry on walking to safety)

● Gloves and face shield

INDIVIDUAL MEDICATION It is important to know the medical requirements of all group members and to ensure that sufficient supplies of medications are carried for the trip (including extra in case conditions delay return times).

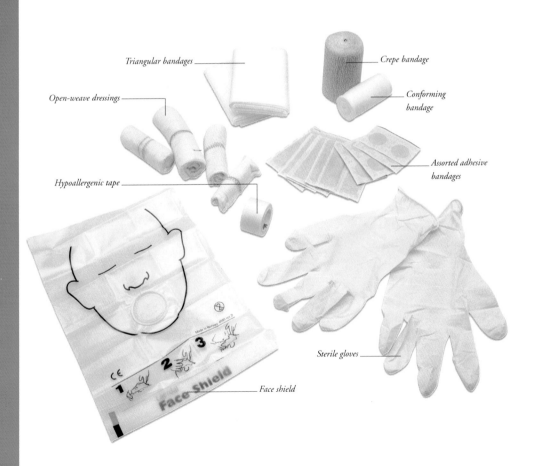

Triangular bandages

Open-weave dressings

Hypoallergenic tape

Crepe bandage

Conforming bandage

Assorted adhesive bandages

Sterile gloves

Face shield

Observation Chart/ Victim Record

When help arrives it is important to pass on as much accurate information as possible. This will enable the professionals to make a swift assessment of the victim's condition and to decide on the next most appropriate course of action. While waiting for help to arrive, make regular checks on the patient and, if circumstances allow, record your findings.

An observation chart/victim record has two main purposes:

● To provide information to the health professionals to help them to make an accurate diagnosis of the victim's condition. The Glasgow Coma Scale is a widely used score that helps to provide information on whether a victim's condition is improving or deteriorating over time.

● To meet legal requirements.
If you are acting as a first responder in the workplace or in any other formal setting, check the recording requirements of your role.

 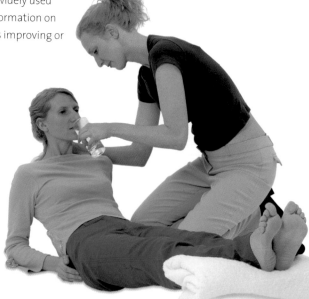

Right
Check on progress at regular intervals, keep the victim comfortable, and offer reassurance.

Date ....

Brief history of incident ....

....

Brief details of the victim's signs, symptoms, and medical history ....

....

Name of victim ....

Brief details of treatment given ....

....

GLASGOW COMA SCALE (Measuring the level of response)
Put the appropriate score in the column after each check

Record at 10 minute intervals		10	20	30	40
Eyes	Open spontaneously 4				
	Open to speech 3				
	Open to pain 2				
	No response 1				
Speech	Responds clearly to questions 5				
	Seems confused 4				
	Responds inappropriately 3				
	Incomprehensible sounds 2				
	No response 1				
Movement	Obeys commands 6				
	Points to pain 5				
	Moves from pain 4				
	Bends in response to pain 3				
	Stretches in response to pain 2				
	No response 1				
	Total (out of 15)				

RECORDING PULSE AND BREATHING RATES (Where possible record pulse and breathing rates every 10 minutes.)

Record at 10 minute intervals	10	20	30	40
Pulse rate—beats per minute				
Description (weak, strong, regular, irregular)				
Breathing—breaths per minute				
Description (noisy, quiet)				

CONTACT DETAILS OF FIRST RESPONDER
You may wish to include your contact details in case medical staff have questions on the scene, care of the victim, or the victim's condition that may help with the diagnosis and treatment of the victim. ....

....

Storing and Using Medication

Not counting the medical products that are available over-the-counter from pharmacies, there are several thousand different preparations that your doctor could prescribe for you. Each of these drugs will have cost millions of dollars during development, and will also have been subjected to rigorous examination by the Food and Drug Agency (FDA).

Right
When storing medication at home it is best to keep them all in one place, ideally in a lockable wall cabinet. It should be in a dry, cool place, out of the reach of children.

STORING DRUGS Most drugs can be stored at room temperature, but there are a few that should be placed in a refrigerator. Drugs in this category include some eye and ear drops and insulin (used to treat diabetes). All other drugs should be locked away out of the reach of children. If several members of the household are taking medication on a regular basis, each person should store his drugs separately.

TAKING MEDICATION It is vital to read the instructions advising how a drug should be taken before the first dose is administered. Although some medication still comes in small, childproof bottles labeled with dosage and special instructions or precautions, many now come as a standard manufacturer's pack. This pack will, by law, contain a leaflet advising the dose to be taken as well as all aspects of special instructions, side effects, and guidance on dealing with accidental overdose. If the instructions are still not clear, seek advice from your pharmacist or doctor.

COMPLETING THE COURSE There are a number of instructions that are common to several groups of drugs. In the case of antibiotics, short courses of steroids, and drugs to cure stomach ulcers it is essential that the full course of the medication is taken. This is to ensure that the complete effect of the drug is experienced, because symptoms will often go half-way through treatment. If medication is stopped early, partially treated conditions are likely to recur.

Similarly, many drugs for the treatment of long-standing conditions, including diabetes, high blood pressure, heart disease, high cholesterol, or asthma should not be stopped by a patient unless he has been instructed to do so by a doctor. Some of these medical problems, in particular, high blood pressure and high cholesterol, have no symptoms but are being treated to reduce the risk of future heart attacks and strokes. A patient who stops taking prescribed drugs in these conditions will not be fully aware of the potential dangers he is facing because he will feel well.

TAKING DIFFERENT MEDICATION Many people have to take a number of different drugs every day. Generally, it is safe to take a variety of medications at the same time, but there are some groups that should be kept apart if possible because they might interfere with the way the drugs are absorbed in the stomach. When in doubt, ask your pharmacist for help. Always tell your doctor or pharmacist if you are taking any over-the-counter or complementary therapies for your condition.

DRIVING There are several classes of medication that may cause drowsiness or sedation, and it is important that a person taking these types of drugs should not drive. Among the remedies that can have this effect are some antihistamines (for allergy), strong analgesics, and antidepressants. The sedative effect of these drugs can be made worse by alcohol, which should be avoided.

Commonly Prescribed Drugs: What They Do and Side Effects

Every day in the US, medication costing millions of dollars is prescribed to hundreds of thousands of people. There are thousands of different drugs used to treat hundreds of illnesses. What follows is a general guide to some of the broad categories of medication, how they work, and common side effects.

ANALGESICS (PAINKILLERS) Acetaminophen and aspirin are the mildest analgesics, used for headaches, joint pains, menstrual pain, and toothache. They are equally effective, but aspirin also reduces inflammation. Acetaminophen can be used in children under the age of twelve. Side effects are rare, but it is potentially fatal even in minor overdose because of toxic effects on the liver. Side effects of aspirin and other anti-inflammatories (e.g. ibuprofen) include stomach irritation and bleeding. Asthma

THE EFFECT OF ANALGESICS

Strong analgesics known as opioids, derived from opium, are used to relieve severe pain. Pain is transmitted in signals along nerves from the source of pain to the brain, where it passes from one brain cell to another until it reaches the part of the brain that interprets the signal as pain. Opioid analgesics block the transmission of the nerve impulses in the brain, reducing the sensation of pain.

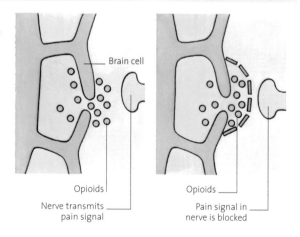

Brain cell

Opioids

Nerve transmits pain signal

Opioids

Pain signal in nerve is blocked

sufferers can be sensitive to aspirin, leading to increased wheezing, and even death in some cases. Stronger analgesics work on the brain to reduce the perception of pain. These include opioid analgesics, such as codeine, pethidine, and morphine. Side effects include drowsiness, constipation, nausea, and vomiting.

HEART DISEASE There are around ten different classes of drugs used to treat a variety of conditions, including high blood pressure, blood clots, angina, and palpitations. The best known of the drugs are water tablets (diuretics). They remove excess fluid from the circulatory system, lowering blood pressure and improving breathing in heart failure. Side effects include stomach upsets, gout, and rashes.

Beta-blockers reduce heart rate and lower blood pressure, but can cause tiredness, cold hands and feet, and sleep disturbances. They should not be taken by asthmatics because they may trigger a fatal attack of wheezing. Digoxin is used to treat irregular heart rate and may induce nausea, vomiting, and loss of appetite if the dosage is too high. Some drugs used for treating raised blood pressure can cause impotence (reversible on stopping medication).

ASTHMA There are two types of asthma therapy. Treatment of wheezing attacks is by inhaled drugs, including salbutamol and terbutaline (known as relievers), which open up the airways by relaxing the muscle in the walls of breathing tubes. Preventatives, such

HOW ANTACIDS WORK

Acid in digestive juices may inflame the lining of the stomach and irritate the stomach walls. Antacids are used to relieve indigestion or help stomach ulcers to heal. They are mild alkaline substances taken orally that neutralize acidity in the digestive juices, allowing eroded areas in the mucus membrane lining the stomach to recover.

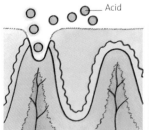

Digestive juices in the stomach contain acid, which may eat away at the mucus layer and inflame the stomach lining.

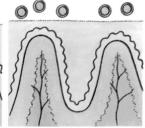

The antacid combines with stomach acid and neutralizes it, reducing irritation and giving the mucus membrane time to heal.

as inhaled steroids, improve breathing by reducing the amount of sticky mucus blocking the airways. Inhaled drugs have few side effects, although steroids can cause an overgrowth of yeast infection at the back of the throat.

DEPRESSION All drugs for depression work by affecting neurotransmitters, chemicals in the brain that pass signals between nerves. These neurotransmitters are low in depressed individuals. Older drugs called tricyclics work mainly on noradrenalin. Side effects include drowsiness, agitation, dry mouth, constipation, blurred vision, and retention of urine.

Newer drugs, such as Prozac, raise the levels of serotonin to improve symptoms. They may cause nausea, agitation, loss of appetite, and sweating. Antidepressants take two to four weeks to have an effect, and should always be withdrawn slowly.

STOMACH PROBLEMS Many stomach problems, including ulcers, heartburn, and indigestion, are caused by excess acid in the stomach. The simplest drugs used to treat symptoms are antacids, which neutralize stomach acid. These drugs can form a raft on top of the stomach contents, preventing backflow from the stomach into the esophagus.

More advanced drugs reduce acid production by blocking the action of nerves supplying acid-producing glands in the lining of the stomach (H_2 blockers), or by acting

HOW BRONCHODILATORS WORK

Bronchodilators widen the airways of the lungs to ease breathing difficulties caused by conditions such as asthma. Before inhaling the drug, the airways become abnormally narrowed as the muscles in their walls contract.

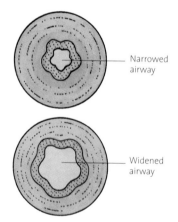

Narrowed airway

Widened airway

Bronchodilators relieve wheezing, tight chest, and shortness of breath by acting on nerve endings in the muscles in the walls of the airways. The muscles relax and the airways widen, increasing airflow in the lungs.

on the acid pump within the cells of these glands (proton pump inhibitors). These drugs have few side effects, and work so well that it is difficult to persuade patients to stop taking them.

Drug Interactions

Drug interactions may occur when a person takes two or more drugs at the same time. The drugs might be given for the same condition, for example, high blood pressure, or the person may have more than one illness requiring treatment. The effect of the interaction can vary from increased side effects from one of the drugs to loss of effectiveness of any of the medicines involved in the interaction.

HOW DRUGS WORK To understand how these interactions occur, it is essential to know what happens to a drug after it is swallowed, the most common way of taking medication. Generally, the drug reaches the stomach and is absorbed through the stomach wall into the bloodstream. Once in the blood, most molecules of the drug are carried along, loosely connected to proteins, until they reach their target tissues. Many drugs work by linking up to specific proteins called receptors on the surface of cells.

When the drug has performed its function, it has to be removed from the body. Most drugs are broken down in the liver and then eliminated from the bloodstream by the kidneys, which filter the remnants of the drug into the urine.

Interactions can occur in a number of ways, with the end result that either too high a level of medication is found in the blood, leading to increased side effects, or too little of the drug is present and it will not work effectively.

TYPES OF INTERACTION Two drugs taken at the same time may affect the same receptor site on the cell surface. The medication that has the strongest attraction to the receptor will prevent the other drug from having an effect. Alternatively, one drug may interfere with the effectiveness of another, either delaying or reducing it. Delayed absorption rarely has serious consequences, but reduced absorption makes a drug less effective.

Many drugs can increase the levels of the enzymes in the liver responsible for breaking down other drugs taken at the same time. This leads to lower concentrations of the affected medication in the blood, reducing its potency. This action is known as enzyme induction. When the drug causing the induction is withdrawn, levels of the second drug can increase dramatically, causing harmful effects.

SERIOUS INTERACTIONS Many drug interactions are harmless, and even those that are potentially more serious will only occur in a

HOW A DRUG WORKS

A drug taken orally reaches the stomach and is absorbed through the stomach walls into the bloodstream and carried to target tissues. It then has to be removed from the body, and is broken down in the liver and eliminated by the kidneys.

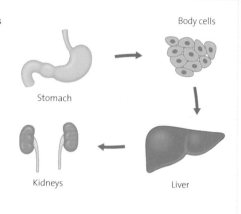

Body cells

Stomach

Kidneys

Liver

small minority of patients. However, there is a number of more serious interactions, involving commonly prescribed drugs, which are important. Some of the most significant follow.

The effectiveness of the oral contraceptive pill can be reduced by antibiotics and some drugs for epilepsy. Warfarin, a drug commonly used for thinning the blood, can be affected by some antibiotics, analgesics, drugs used to treat cholesterol, and epilepsy drugs. Antidepressants and tranquilizers are among the drugs acting on the central nervous system. They can have their sedative effects increased by some of the stronger analgesics available.

These are just a few of the hundreds of possible interactions that can take place. It would be very difficult for individual doctors to know all potential interactions, but almost all doctors use computers to generate prescriptions, and many of these interactions are highlighted by the computer system.

Interactions can also take place between prescription medicines and those bought over-the-counter from a pharmacist. This also applies to herbal medicines and homeopathic preparations. It is important to inform your doctor if you are taking any such medicines because it may influence her prescribing decision.

DRUG ROUTES INTO THE BODY

There are a number of ways of introducing drugs into the body. Most drugs are taken orally in the form of pills, capsules, or liquids. Intravenous injection enables a drug to take effect very quickly because it enters the bloodstream and is circulated to the part of the body where it is needed. Drugs act in a variety of ways. Some simply kill off invading organisms such as bacteria, viruses, and fungi. Others alter the effects of body chemicals. Some may affect a part of the nervous system that controls a particular process.

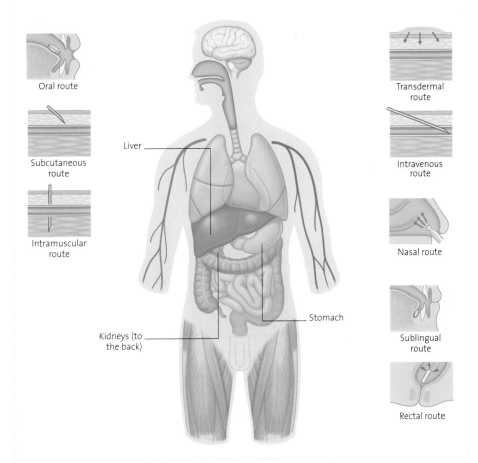

Oral route

Subcutaneous route

Intramuscular route

Liver

Kidneys (to the back)

Stomach

Transdermal route

Intravenous route

Nasal route

Sublingual route

Rectal route

The Complementary Medicine Chest

A growing number of people use complementary remedies to treat everyday illnesses and minor accidents. These can also be used at home to speed recovery after first aid treatment, to relieve pain, and to calm the mind. This section gives an overview of some popular therapies, discusses what conditions they may be suitable for, and some remedies likely to be found in the home.

A BALANCED APPROACH Most complementary practitioners treat the patient as a whole rather than just treating the physical symptoms of an illness. Emotional and spiritual health are considered to be just as important as physical health, and all need to be in a state of balance for a person to be truly well. The aim of treatment is to encourage the patient's powers of self-healing.

A first consultation is likely to take at least an hour as the practitioner builds up a complete picture to determine your condition and the appropriate remedy. You will be asked questions concerning medical history, diet, and lifestyle and perhaps your moods, likes, and dislikes. The number of sessions usually depends on the nature of the condition. Always inform your doctor if you are having this treatment because some medicines may interact with complementary remedies.

Complementary remedies are readily available from health food stores and pharmacies, but like their prescription counterparts should always be kept out of the reach of children because they may contain harmful ingredients.

AROMATHERAPY Aromatherapy is a type of herbal medicine that uses concentrated plant essences known as essential oils to improve physical and emotional health. Essential oils are massaged into the skin or inhaled through the nose, and molecules within them enter the bloodstream. Scents released by the oils act on certain parts of the brain and in theory an aroma might affect stress levels, mood, metabolism, and libido.

Most essential oils are extracted by steam distillation. Plant material is heated until it vaporizes. The essential oil floats on top and is skimmed off and bottled. The most common form of aromatherapy is to massage diluted oils (combined with carrier oils such as almond or sunflower) into the skin. Inhalations are thought to be highly effective because smell receptors in the nose have direct links with the brain. Vaporizers and scented baths are also popular.

Left
*A well-stocked
complentary medicine
chest might include:
herbal remedies such as
echinacea, comfrey,
St. John's wort; essential
oils such as lavender, tea
tree, and eucalyptus;
Bach's rescue remedy and
various homeopathic
preparations.*

Aromatherapy is mainly used to treat stress-related conditions such as headache, anxiety, depression, and sleeplessness. Various oils may also be beneficial for digestive complaints (including indigestion, flatulence, and diarrhea); muscular aches and pains; skin problems such as acne, burns, stings, and eczema; problems such as cystitis and yeast infection; and respiratory disorders (including coughs, colds, sinusitis, and catarrh). Useful oils to have in stock include lavender, tea tree, eucalyptus, peppermint, rosemary, sandalwood, and clary sage. Pay attention to instructions for dilution, and note that many oils are unsuitable for use on children. Some oils are unsafe to use during pregnancy or if you suffer from high blood pressure, and use inhalations with care if you have asthma or are prone to nosebleeds.

BACH FLOWER REMEDIES These remedies were developed in the 1930s by Dr. Edward Bach, who believed that flowers possessed healing properties that could be used to treat emotional problems and restore physical and mental well-being. Dr. Bach identified seven emotional categories (fearfulness, uncertainty, lack of interest in present circumstances, loneliness, over-sensitivity, despair and despondency, and over-concern for others' well-being), under which he grouped 38 remedies, which were developed primarily for self-help use.

Flower remedies are made by infusing or boiling plant material in spring water then preserving in alcohol, and are now available from all over the world. They are mainly used for dealing with emotional problems and stress. The compound Rescue Remedy is taken for shock, panic, and hysteria, and is often found in the home.

HERBALISM Herbal remedies have been used for thousands of years throughout the world to treat disease and promote well-being. Many pharmaceutical drugs, such as aspirin and digoxin, are derived from isolated plant extracts, but herbalists believe that the therapeutic effects of plants are greater when the whole plant is used.

Wild herbs are dried and processed under strict conditions to form a variety of pills, syrups, infusions, creams, and ointments. Many of these preparations are now available from health food stores and pharmacies. Often, herbal medicines contain a number of herbs, each effective at relieving one particular symptom of an illness.

Herbal remedies are used for a variety of conditions including stress, fatigue, sleep disturbance, coughs and colds, skin complaints, and menopausal symptoms. They should be avoided in pregnancy and during breastfeeding unless specific advice regarding safety has been obtained from a trained herbalist. Care should be taken if suffering from high blood pressure, diabetes, epilepsy, heart disease, or glaucoma. Useful herbal preparations for the home include comfrey, marigold, echinacea, St. John's wort, feverfew, slippery elm, dong quai (for women), oil of evening primrose, ginseng, valerian, and chamomile. Herbal treatments are not free from side effects, and may interact with conventional medication. It is essential that you inform your herbalist and your doctor of any preparations being taken.

HOMEOPATHY This is a popular system of medicine based on the principle of "like cures like," meaning that the treatment is similar in substance to the illness it is relieving. The theory is that many symptoms experienced during an illness are a consequence of the body's own defense mechanisms attempting to cure the disease. By giving a substance that mimics the illness, the body's ability to fight off the condition is boosted.

Homeopathic remedies are derived from many sources—vegetable, plant, and mineral—and are prepared by making a solution of the original substance and diluting it, a process known as potentization. The remedy is shaken rapidly after each dilution. One drop of the original solution is added to 99 drops of water and this solution has a potency of 1c. One drop of a 1c solution is then diluted again with 99 drops of water to produce a solution with a 2c strength, and so on. Most remedies are 6c or 30c potency.

According to homeopathic theory, the more diluted the remedy, the more potent it is considered to be. It seems likely that by the time the most dilute solutions are made up, there will be virtually no active ingredient left, and there is a theory that the water used to dilute the substance retains an imprint of the active ingredient, allowing it to exert its therapeutic effect. This theory is still open to debate but there is mounting evidence that homeopathy is safe, and can be an effective therapy for a wide range of conditions, often used with conventional medical treatment. Many homeopathic practitioners are also medically qualified.

Homeopathy can be used to treat a range of physical and psychological complaints, such as coughs and colds; digestive disorders; asthma and allergies; burns, cuts, and bruises; skin rashes; menstrual and menopausal problems; anxiety and mild depression. Basic remedies, in the form of pills, ointments, and tinctures, are readily available in pharmacies and health food stores and can be used for simple maladies and first aid. Long-standing conditions such as eczema are best treated by individual remedies prescribed by a qualified homeopath.

Homeopathic remedies kept at home might include arnica, aconite, apis, carbo veg., graphites, hypericum, pulsatilla, sulphur, and silica. When taking pills, do not touch them: tap them out into the container lid or onto a clean teaspoon. Symptoms may briefly worsen after you start treatment, thought to be an effect of your immune system becoming activated. Remedies should be stored in tightly sealed containers in a cool, dark place, away from essential oils and perfumes.

NATUROPATHY Naturopathy, or natural medicine, first developed in the late 19th century, and was based on ancient beliefs in the ability of the body to heal itself, given the right circumstances. It is a multi-disciplinary approach that uses noninvasive therapies to improve underlying health so that the patient is less susceptible to infection, rather than treating symptoms directly. The most commonly used therapies include nutrition (including vitamin and mineral supplementation) and fasting, hydrotherapy, massage, osteopathy, herbalism, homeopathy, relaxation therapies, yoga, and counseling. The aim is to support what is termed the "triad of health"—the body's musculoskeletal system, its internal biochemistry, and emotional well-being.

A naturopath may use a wide range of tests to build up a picture of your physical and emotional well-being. Tests may include a routine medical, X-rays, blood tests, and sweat or hair analysis. Treatment is tailored to the individual's needs and will be catabolic (cleansing, to eliminate toxins) or anabolic (aiming to build up the system).

Naturopathy may be particularly beneficial for relieving stress and depression, tiredness, high blood pressure, digestive problems, skin conditions, asthma, and arthritis. Many of the principles advocated by naturopaths, such as the importance of regular exercise and a healthy diet, drinking plenty of water, and deep breathing, have long been part of mainstream medical advice.

IN THE PANTRY Different foods have been used for centuries to treat illness and maintain good health. Sometimes considered a part of folk medicine, the traditional beliefs, practises, and materials used in every culture that are designed to maintain well-being and fight disease in the absence of conventional medicine. Advice has been handed down from generation to generation to promote healing by supporting underlying good health, and is still used today because it works. Common conditions that respond well to home treatment include headaches, stress, anxiety and depression, respiratory disorders, skin problems, digestive problems, some forms of arthritis, premenstrual syndrome, and menopause. Minor first aid conditions such as small burns, cuts, bruises, stings, and sprains can also be safely treated. Serious disorders require medical attention.

Many common foodstuffs used to protect against illness are now being shown to have beneficial effects for health. Garlic, for example, may reduce levels of unhealthy cholesterol in the blood. Food can also be safely used with conventional medicine.

Traditional home remedies include onions for gastric infections, circulatory disorders, bronchitis and boils; garlic for respiratory and circulatory problems; and cabbage poultices to relieve the pain and inflammation of arthritis and to alleviate swollen, tender breasts in nursing mothers. Honey is taken to soothe sore throats or added to water to treat conjunctivitis. Lemon juice fights infection, yogurt treats yeast infection, cranberry juice is a urinary system bactericide and treatment for cystitis. Apply vinegar to stings to reduce swelling; add mustard powder to a footbath to treat colds and headaches; rub olive oil into the scalp to reduce flaking. For sore, irritated eyes, a slice of cucumber or a cold teabag on each eyelid will reduce swelling. To alleviate a hangover, many people swear by eating a grapefruit.

Index

Bold page numbers indicate main references.

Addresses

First Aid

Kids Health
12735 W. Grand Bay Parkway
Jacksonville, FL 32258
Phone: 904-288-5750
http://kidshealth.org/parent/firstaid_safe/index.html

Walgreens.com
First Aid & Emergency Care
Toll Free: 877-250-5823
www.walgreens.com/library/firstaid

General Information

American Medical Association
515 N. State Street
Chicago, IL 60610
Phone: 312-474-5000
www.ama-assn.org

The US Department of Health and
Human Services
200 Independence Avenue
SW Washington, DC 20201
Toll Free: 877-696-6775
Phone: 202-619-0257
www.os.dhhs.gov

Acknowledgments

Special thanks are due to the models who participated in the studio photography; Anita Kerwin-Nye and Gloria Moss of the Red Cross UK, Sussex Branch, for the provision of a first aid trainer and equipment; Paul Clayton of J. S. Clayton Ltd for the loan of first aid kits; The Outdoor Centre, Lewes, East Sussex, UK, for the loan of outdoor and camping equipment.